The Remembering

SAHARRA WHITE-WOLF

Illustrations by: **Martin Mancha**

Library of Congress Control Number: 2018942459
          Paperback: 978-1-948817-50-9
          eBook: 978-1-948817-52-3
          Hardcover: 978-1-948817-51-6

BOOK-ART
PRESS SOLUTIONS

30 Wall Street, 8th Floor
New York City, NY 10005
www.bookartpress.us
+1-800-351-3529

*This book is dedicated
to my mother Elisabeth Eile
and my grandparents
Richard and Friderike Findenig*

Contents

Foreword

Dear Children,

I am thanking you and/or the adult who picked up this book for you. I am excited to be part of your life as we are going to be on this journey of ReMembering together. This book is quantum based, meaning there is no time.

I would like to tell you how it all unfolded for me, as it is important, I feel, for you to know.

It all started around three years ago, when spirit asked me to start writing my first book. Well, I resisted and had my own self-doubt about if I would be a good enough writer. I have never written anything, at least in this life, and English is not my mother tongue.

After a while though, I thought that writing fairy tales, based on my own shamanic experience with spirit, would be feasible. I was getting excited about inspiring children, like YOU, and adults to explore the unseen world of spirit and to conquer their own self-doubts and shadows to find out that self-love and compassion are the only tools we need besides staying in the "NOW".

So, the first book was created, "The Inside World". Spirit and I wrote the book in six weeks. After it was published, my Higher Self told me that 'The Inside World" is going to be the first book of "The Inner Knowing Trilogy".

After writing my first book, I was on a deep inner journey of expanding consciousness; meaning to explore the inner world of mine and who I truly was. Little did I know that I had started the journey of my second book "The Remembering".

If you would have told me two years ago that we are Star Beings and can communicate with Cosmic Beings, I would have said, "yeah, right!". At that time, I was not yet aware of this. But spirit had its own way with me and I always listen to my Higher Self with a discerning heart. The heart is the compass and will always give us the right answer in the "NOW".

I was guided to attend a Light Language Ceremony in Pennsylvania with an Andara Spiral event. I have explored many different kinds of Ceremonies in my last two decades and have facilitated several different kinds myself. This one was very unique and unusual. People were speaking different languages of the Stars, and although I could not understand anything, I knew that the energies were very high frequency and activated me. Three days later, I started speaking the Cosmic Language of Light myself. There have been many people who have been speaking this Language of Light for decades. I am very new to this and maybe you are speaking it already, and you did not realize what you were doing. I am here to tell you that you are not crazy.

The Language of Light is not linear in structure: meaning you cannot learn it word by word. It is channeled and gets you out of the left brain (logical thinking) into the right brain (love-based thinking) and activates the parts of your brain, which we are not using yet. I experienced that the Language of Light works on DNA activation and unites us with the Cosmic Heart: the high love frequencies of the Stars. It brought awareness to my multidimensional parts and started me on a journey of deep soul-remembering.

Suddenly I remembered the Cosmos and that I was from the Stars. I remembered Lemurian lives and what I did. On one side it was exciting and blissful and on the other side this realization came with a deep feeling of sadness for being away from my soul star family for such a long time. At least that's what happened to me and what I have witnessed with others as well. Since then, a lot has changed. I am now facilitating Cosmic Light Language Ceremonies and I love it. Holding this kind of Cosmic Ceremony is truly one of my passions and part of my life. I became aware that after my almost twenty years of being involved in energy and shamanic work, that I do not need to learn anything anymore, rather unlearn. I came to the understanding that the energies on New Earth work differently. I realized that all is within me; I just have to show up, trust that I will know in every moment what I need to be doing, because I have done it before in many lives. All is divine, all is perfect and for me at least benevolent.

From my first book "The Inside World", Master Merlin and Novix were mentioned who were my Spirit Guides at that time. Novix and many of my Native American Guides have moved on since then. I decided to keep Novix in this book though. Master Merlin is still working with me and wants to teach me Alchemy. Well, he needs patience with me because I am not getting his symbolism yet.

Although this is a New Age Fiction Story or Cosmic Fairy Tale, I am here to tell you that the Spirit Guides of Ronja and Sarah are the ones I am working with at the moment. This book is based on my life. Sarah represents my 3D worldly experience, as well as Ronja and my multidimensional Guides or Selves if you want to call it as such.

I am working with Dhalia, my Pleiadian Guide, Buddha Ganesh, the mayor of Inner Earth, Fiandra, my Sirian twin flame, Tartan, the Mountain Being who guides me with grid work, Nilem is actually another Merlin in my life, who is blind and helps me with feeling states in the Quantum Field. Several of my experiences in deep meditation or in our light language meditation calls are in this book, from the Sirian to the Central Sun experience etc.

The Lemurian Council of the Cosmic Heart & Light are the ones I am channeling. They are Pleiadians, Sirians and Arcturians. This book "The Remembering" is a Pleiadian Transmission, meaning you will receive Pleiadian energies while reading it. Whereas the third one will be a Sirian Transmission. The Emerald Green Circle of the Stars, who I am guided to work with at the moment, will find its place in my third book. The third book of "The Inner Knowing Trilogy" will be called "The Revolution" and will be future based.

It might be very exciting for you to hear that the Lemurian Star Team truly exists. Rosemary Healy is Valerie, Vincent Braccia is Kai, Nina is Karen Cressman, Todd is BobbyLight and Olivia is Patricia Miller.

By the way: We, the Lemurian Star Team, are always up for a new adventure. We can travel to your area for Cosmic Light Language Ceremonies and sacred Lemurian & Quantum Healing Retreats. Please contact Rosemary at rohealy999@gmail.com.

Just in case if you are curious, Ezrael does exist. He is not aware of it yet and maybe never will. This is not for me to share. The remembering process is something that cannot be forced. It comes in its own time when we are ready for it.

This book is very dear to me as it entails the written Cosmic Language of Light, which is for me my mother tongue. Spirit and I wrote this book in 5 weeks. Almost every day, I got woken up at around 3:33 am to work on this book and so we did. Everything just evolved very fast from there and I was committed. Rosemary and I edited the book almost every day and we truly felt the energies of the book and that we were getting activated by it. We also had a lot of fun. It was a beautiful experience working with her. I listened to only one song continuously while writing this book. The song is called "Adiemus" from the album "Songs of Sanctuary" by Karl Jenkins. Check it out, if you want to explore the feeling state of my writing experience.

Have I experienced dark entities in my life and interference you might wonder? Yes, I did. These dark forces are represented by Imero. As there is dark there is light. We need both of it and it is just a matter of balancing the two. Love and Light through compassion are all we can ask for and will always prevail. Demand divine intervention whenever you need it. We are far more powerful than we think or than authority makes us believe.

In my perspective the biggest enemy we have is ourselves. Our negative self-talk, mostly because of our own imprints from family, society, school etc. we create our "filtered" reality.

After this book was finished, Occuna came to me in one of my meditations by surprise. He showed himself to me as my shadow, the dark parts of myself I was not aware of at the moment, and my ego. Both just wanted to be heard, felt and seen. I did the same that Serenata did in this book and felt lighter afterwards. I was excited that I actually experienced a part of my book after it was written. There we go again: this book is quantum.

We all have shadow and we all have light. We are holding the divine masculine and feminine within us. All is paired in two, and All is ONE in the eyes of the Cosmic Heart. WE ARE DIVINE!

Dear children of the Earth,

I am here to tell you that we need YOU to stay awake and that your laughter, your innocence, your imagination, your wisdom, your unconditional love and your connection to Mother Gaia & Spirit are important for the Evolution of this Planet.

You have chosen to be here to bring in your power, your gifts and your remembering from the Stars to help Humanity evolve. We need YOU and YOU are important.

Never underestimate what your imagination and laughter do for this planet, it is all quantum based: meaning it goes everywhere: past, present, future - everywhere!!!

There will come the time when we will learn from YOU, dear children.

- *I am here to stand for YOU.*

- *I am here to honor YOU for who you truly are.*

- *I am here to invite you to envision humanity living in Peace, in alignment with Mother Gaia and that this change will come with Ease and Grace.*

- *Envision with me: people working together with joy, who found God within themselves; and with that kindness, compassion and integrity.*

- *Envision with me clean waters. Every child being protected and everyone has food to eat and clean water to drink.*

- *I am inviting you to envision this with me daily and offer cornmeal, tobacco or your laughter to Mother Earth and to our Ancestors.*

- *Find your way into sacred Ceremony if you are called to do so.*

- *Take care of Mother Earth and honor her. She needs our love and appreciation as well. Clean up the Earth after yourself and after others who forgot to do so.*

- *Find your connection to your Higher Self, your God-connection, it will never lead you astray.*

- *Trust your INNER KNOWING and be aware that nobody can take this away from you.*

- *Be patient with us adults, we did not have the privilege to grow up in a higher consciousness state as you.*

- *I am here to tell you that your innocence, your heart, your imagination and your positive thoughts are the keys for the Ascension of this Planet.*

- *Please believe in yourself, love and honor yourself, conquer your self-doubt and connect with like-minded people to find God within you.*

- *Become everything and nothing and omnipresence will be the gift you receive.*

- *Demand divine intervention and ask for help when you need it. We are the Planet of free choice. All you need to do is to ask for the highest good, from a space of compassion and interconnectedness, and you shall receive.*

Aho! And so it is!

I am not here to put my belief system on you. This is not my intention. Rather, I want to inspire you to go on your own inward spiritual journey to find out what is true for you and to step out of the box/the matrix of the mind. You will find many tools to use in this book. Maybe it is your turn to pick up these tools. Enjoy the journey of ReMembering and Thank you for reading.

Madaaheta aka! Godnaneta ubanda godoheda madaga!

WE are but ONE and it is time to REMEMBER and to COME TOGETHER AS ONE.

I love you!

NAMASTE

Saharra

Acknowledgement

Deepest gratitude for my children Yonas, Yana and Yarina. I would not be who I am without you. I love you so much!

I want to thank from the bottom of my heart, Rosemary Healy, who did the amazing editing for this book with me. You are truly a wonderful friend and a gift to me. It was so much fun working with you.

Thank you, Martin Mancha, for your amazing, powerful work and fast delivery of the illustrations. You are a very talented artist. I am wishing you all the best on your endeavors.

Thank you, Ori Rennick, my Lemurian soul sister, for all your excitement in helping with the corrections. Thank you for your Love.

Dearest Melissa Goldstein, thank you for being the angel again and helping me with the last corrections. Thank you for your love and kindness.

A big Thank you to Patricia Miller and Eva Franco for proof reading my book so fast.

Thank you! Thank you! Thank you to the Lemurian Star Team:

Rosemary Healy (Valerie): Thank you for always thinking outside of the box and making the impossible possible. Thank you for your talent and sharing with us new ways of how to play in the Quantum Field. Your continuous effort to serve the planet is truly inspiring. I am looking forward to witnessing your new adventures ahead.

Vince Braccia (Kai): you are born with unity consciousness and thank you for all your continuous support and willingness to shift this planet to a better world with your dragon magic and your grid work. Thank you for always helping out. (www.skyseedenergy.com)

Patricia Miller (Olivia): thank you for your care and ongoing support. I am excited about your Mayan remembering. Can't wait to see what will come next for you besides your amazing cooking adventure. (www.spiritflightsacredjourney.com and www.bluemoonculinary.com)

BobbyLight (Todd): Thank you for your kindness and your Love and Light. Thank you for bringing the crystal skulls together for healing. I can't wait to see where it goes with that. (BobbyLight Rowlands on facebook)

Karen Cressman (Nina): thank you for being a Seer and spreading the word of the Cosmos through the Andromeda Council and your other journey podcasts with us. All the best on your endeavors and thank you for the beacon of light that you are. (www.KarenCressman.com)

I am so glad you all landed divinely in this book.

Thank you to the beautiful members of our daily Light Language Meditation call group: Rosemary, Ori, Pat, Kyra, Phillip, Tom Williams, Hawk, Anca, Markus, Fran, Victoria, Rachel, Mark, Oleg, Agnes, Joyce, Peggy, Eva, Billy, Laura, Barbara, Lois and all the other ones who hop in from time to time.

A big Thank you goes to Valerie Eagle Heart Meyer and her amazing community. Your prayer dance has changed my life forever.

I am deeply grateful for my amazing Hospice team. How blessed I am to work with such compassionate people.

Thank you Nahko for giving me permission to use your Direction song for this book in audio for free. I love your music and your message.

Thank you to the Creator, my Cosmic Guides, my Guardians, my Ancestors, Mother Earth and to unconditional Love. I am deeply grateful that I had the chance to experience so much magic already in my life. I feel so much gratitude for being able to feel compassion and love on New Earth in a way like never before. I know that this is just the beginning for all of us.

Gratitude to all my communities and people who have touched my heart. I could go on and on with all of your names. Please know that even if you are not mentioned, you are in my heart.

BLACK WRITING: THE STORY TAKES PLACE IN OUR 3D WORLD, WHICH WE SEE WITH OUR EYES RIGHT IN FRONT OF US

BLUE WRITING: THE STORY TAKES PLACE IN THE MULTIDIMENSIONAL SPIRIT WORLDS: THE UNSEEN WORLDS

PURPLE WRITING: THE STORY TAKES PLACE IN THE INSIDE WORLDS: THE PLACE WHERE THE SPIRIT OF HUMAN MERGES WITH THE MULTIDIMENSIONAL WORLDS, SPIRIT GUIDES AND LIGHT BEINGS. THESE WORLDS AND BEINGS WE CAN SEE WITH OUR INNER EYE

CHAPTER 1

The Remembering

Ronja awoke from a recurrent dream. It was a dream about a boy who continuously struggled with self-doubt and finding his divinity. Many mornings, she woke up worried he would fail, but she trusted that he would find the light within himself and surpass the darkness. The dark forces filled him with self-doubt, which he battled continuously. This time she noticed that the dream was different. He found self-love through compassion for himself. In this process he found infinite power and only light could exist in this frequency.

Ronja jumped up out of bed and shouted out loud full of excitement, "He did it! Oh my God! He did it!" She had dreamt of the boy for so long and had grown to care for him. Although Ronja did not know if he was even real, she did feel in her heart that this boy truly existed and the time would come when they would meet.

Ronja always felt guided by her intuition. It was not something that she had to search for, as it was an "Inner Knowing".

Suddenly, she felt quiet as images from an event, which had occurred three years ago, came into her mind. It was a day that changed her life forever. The girl was surprised that all these memories came up, and she was willing to explore them further.

Ronja laid back down in bed, closed her bright green eyes, and let herself go back in time while feeling unsettled.

It was a Monday. In her vision she was the observer from above watching everything unfold. Her parents had already left for work and Ronja watched herself get ready for school. Her friend Nina rang the doorbell. Nina and Ronja were best friends from the first time they met. They both knew this friendship was destined and honored it. Although both of them had totally different perspectives on life, they felt a heart connection. She was more introverted than Ronja and a great listener.

Ronja recalled her reluctance to go to school that day. She looked at her girlfriend and said, "Nina, I do not know why, but something feels really weird today. It almost seems like I have a premonition that something will happen to me today, that will change my life forever."

Nina looked at Ronja, took her hand and said, "Whatever happens, we will face it together. I won't let you down and maybe doing it together will make it easier for you."

Ronja gave her friend a heartfelt hug and off they went, riding their bikes to school. All the while, Ronja's heart pounded nervously. This feeling increased the closer they came to the school building.

In her first language arts lesson block, Ronja started sweating and shaking. She started crying and could not hold back her tears. Nina was sitting right next to her friend. She was observing Ronja quietly and was holding space for her by breathing in and out softly.

Suddenly, the door opened and the principal walked into the classroom. With a pale face, she looked at the teacher and said, "I am sorry to interrupt the class, but I need to talk to Ronja." Then the principal looked at her and said, "Could you please come with me to my office?"

Usually everyone in the class would laugh out loud in response to this request. However, today total silence was felt in the classroom and everyone stared at Ronja. She was shaking and could not get up. In the next moment, Nina raised her hand and said, "Mrs. Flockner, I would like to help my friend to your office. Actually, I insist on going with Ronja!" Nina was surprised at her own words because usually she was seen as a very shy girl, but something inside of her made her say these words.

The principal hesitated for a moment and then agreed.

For Ronja every step closer to the office made her weaker and weaker. All of a sudden, her grandparents came out of the principal's office. When the grandparents saw Ronja approaching, they walked fast towards her. They both had tears in their eyes and an expression which Ronja had never seen on their faces.

Ronja's grandmother, called Nona, embraced Ronja just as she could not walk anymore. Nona, an older, very wise and elegant looking lady with white, long hair and blue eyes, cried and whispered into Ronja's ears, "My dear Ronja, I need to tell you something, which I wish I would never ever have to tell you."

Ronja could only whisper as she had no strength left in her, "Nona what is it?"

Her grandmother started to cry uncontrollably and said with a shaky voice, "Your parents just passed away in a car accident. It was a tractor trailer accident. I am so sorry, Ronja! I am so sorry!"

In that moment, everything in front of Ronja's eyes turned black and she fell into a deep, deep space.

Ronja saw herself with her parents. Their names were Richard and Frida, the most loving parents a child could wish for. They honored Ronja for her own authentic being and guided her through life instead of putting their requests and thoughts onto her. She was allowed to grow up with her own critical thinking and had the space to experience life. She was allowed to make mistakes, and they were embraced. Her parents knew deep inside of themselves that this was the best way for Ronja to learn. Richard and Frida loved each other so much and Ronja was a creation of their unconditional love. They supported each other in expressing their own individuality, and love was the foundation of their family.

Ronja was delighted to see them. They all were dancing together and the sun was shining on them as the warm breeze of the summer softly stroked their cheeks and hair. Ronja's mom looked at her and said, "Dear daughter, I am so sorry that we had to leave you. This was the contract we agreed on before we came to Earth. We know you do not remember but all is on track. We are needed now on the other side of the veil. This way we can support you best on your mission to help the Earth and the Cosmos. We will always be with you and let ourselves be known through birds, daisies and butterflies. Trust that you will know when we are there for you. It is beautiful here, and do not worry about us. We are in good hands and embraced by God's pure love."

Ronja hugged them and said, "I will miss you very much and yet I know I will get through it. It will take me some time though."

"Yes, love," her father said, "and this dark night of your soul will be the biggest gift in your life. Our energy is within you. We have never left. This is an illusion of your 3D world, Ronja. We will help you remember the magic of the Cosmic Circle of One! Trust that, Ronja!"

The girl continued hugging them and agreed.

After a while, they started walking through a beautiful field of fragrant roses. Ronja thought this was the sweetest smell she had ever experienced. The family walked hand in hand until they reached a beautiful, golden platform with the number 3 written in four corners.

Suddenly a burst of wind came up, and a shadow appeared in front of the sun. The girl looked up and there was a beautiful, large, green dragon flapping his big wings in the air. As soon as he landed, the parents helped Ronja to get onto the dragon. His name was Elmuthan. She had the "Inner Knowing" that this was her dragon.

The parents gave their daughter a farewell kiss and waved Ronja and the dragon goodbye. Ronja and Elmuthan took off through the Cosmos. This was a place that she knew. It was her home. She felt only excitement as she flew through the Stars and the Galaxies again. "Yihiiiiiiiiiiiiiiiiiii!" Ronja screamed from the top of her lungs, full of joy while holding on to her beloved dragon, Elmuthan.

Suddenly, Ronja was not in the Cosmos anymore. Instead she witnessed the scene of herself lying on the floor back in school. Ronja watched Emergency technicians picking her up and taking her to the hospital. From above she could observe everything that was happening to her with ease. It almost seemed like she could be in several places at the same time.

Ronja saw herself lying in a coma for three days. On the third day she opened her eyes but to the surprise of the doctors, the girl could not move nor speak. The physicians went through many tests and even though she was transferred to a specific trauma clinic, nobody could figure out what was causing her condition. She was only able to open her eyes and stare out blankly. All her organs functioned perfectly.

Ronja had a feeding tube inserted to keep her nourished. The doctors told the grandparents that she was in a catatonic state and nobody knew if she would ever recover. The grandparents, still dealing with their own grief and loss of their daughter and son-in-law, decided to take her home. They hired the best health home aide and physiotherapist, who came daily. The therapist moved her joints passively to prevent contraction from happening.

Meanwhile, the grandparents looked for healers over the next few months. They searched all over the world for anyone who might be able to help their grandchild. Shamans and known healers traveled to see Ronja. Some of them were so interested in Ronja's unusual case, they refused to take money; they just wanted to help.

During the entire time Ronja was still able to observe everything from above. From one moment to the next she was back in the Cosmos.

Ronja and Elmuthan were traveling to a very specific star cluster, called "The Seven Sisters", which was the home of the Pleiadians.

They reached one of their planets, Okonis, her friend Dhalia, was waiting for her already. Dhalia was a Pleiadian Priestess. She was part of "The Lemurian Council of the Cosmic Heart & Light", which Ronja had been working with since the beginning of life on Planet Earth. She had beautiful, long, blond hair, and blue eyes. Dhalia was wearing a golden, iridescent, flowy dress. She was more than 7 feet tall.

They greeted each other by lifting their palms to touch and bowing their heads.

Dhalia said, "Welcome cosmic Sister SumuRa, 'Heavenly Dancer of the Sun'. We have awaited you. Please follow me into the docking station. We are getting transported to the Central Sun."

The docking station looked like huge water slides going out into the Cosmos. They walked towards what looked like an elevator door. It opened and both went inside a small space shuttle. They buckled in, the shuttle took off and it became very bumpy. They traveled so quickly that the stars were seen as lines through the Cosmos.

When they arrived at the Central Sun's docking station, the door opened up and they entered a beautiful, golden dome structure. They could see large, golden machines everywhere. They were in the transmission station of the Central Sun, where codes and transmissions were created and sent out to all Universes.

Imukah, the mechanical engineer of the codes and transmissions, welcomed them. He was very happy to see the girl and Dhalia. Imukah was 5 feet tall and very lean. He looked like a humanoid and his face and body were white and appeared to be translucent. Imukah looked old and had a long, white beard.

SumuRa (Ronja) was delighted to see him. She remembered how many visits and work she had done with Imukah at the Central Sun. They greeted each other by touching palms and bowing, as she did prior with Dhalia. This was the general cosmic greeting of the Universe.

In the next moment, SumuRa sat in a chair. She knew what would happen next. A beam of light came from above and below SumuRa's chair and both lights merged and expanded out all around her.

SumuRa closed her eyes and enjoyed the feeling of the energies. These energies, which worked on her pineal gland, were transmissions that would be needed later. The information was stored in her DNA and would be activated on Earth at the right time.

When the transmissions were completed, the beams of light disconnected from each other and all of the light dispersed. SumuRa opened her eyes and expressed gratitude for these downloads. Now it was time to leave.

Dahlia and SumuRa said goodbye to Imukah and went back to the docking station of the Central Sun. They re-entered the space shuttle and returned to the Pleiadian starting point of their journey. Before they said goodbye to each other Dhalia said, "I will be with you in every moment. There will be some difficult times ahead. Trust we are always with you in your heart. We are working with others of your soul group as well and soon you will find each other. It all has been already arranged. Now it is time to go. We will see each other again soon."

They touched palm and bowed heads to say goodbye.

In the next moment, SumuRa was flying back on her dragon Elmuthan and returned to the golden circle, where the journey with her flying friend had started.

Suddenly, Ronja was observing her grandmother looking at the stars. Six months had gone by since Ronja fell into the catatonic state. Tears rolled down her grandmother Nona's face.

She could sense Nona's despair and anger. Losing her daughter and her son-in-law was painful enough and now seeing her granddaughter struggling without any cure was too much for her.

Nona started to weep and fell on her knees on the grass. She could not hold anything back anymore. Nona screamed into the air expressing the sorrow and hopelessness she felt inside of her.

After a while her weeping ceased and she said, "God, I have endured so much and kept the faith even though you took away my dear children. I kept it going for the sake of my granddaughter and my dear, beloved husband. The pain is too much for me to handle. I cannot do it anymore. You need to help me right here and right now!"

She continued to cry out with a stern voice, "You need to send the right healer into my life now! The one who will help my granddaughter wake up! I know you can make this happen. It is time. I need to feel that you truly love me, hear me and will help me!"

Suddenly, a gust of wind came up and she felt that the wind was touching her face and stroking her hair. She felt an invisible but strong presence. In that moment, Nona felt the Oneness with all there is. She looked up and saw a shooting star in the sky while the wind was still blowing. Nona's wind chimes on her porch were beautifully singing with the wind. The grandmother finally felt as if she was heard and this gave her faith. In her perspective, faith was based on belief, versus hope which was based on fear.

For the first time, Nona trusted and expected the most benevolent outcome for Ronja and knew it would be perfect and in divine time. Nona got up, looked at the sky and said, "Thank you God for hearing me! Thank you! Aho and Namaste!" She went back inside and felt as if everything had already been done.

A week later, Nona went to her local health food store to buy some incense, which she could only get at this place. When she entered she saw a woman talking to the cashier. Both were laughing and when this woman laughed, Nona could feel her light. To Nona's surprise she approached the woman and started talking, "I am sorry to interrupt, but I need to ask you a question."

The woman turned towards her. Nona relaxed as she looked into her blue-green eyes that were filled with strength, wisdom and sparkling light. The woman replied, "Sure, how can I help you?"

"My granddaughter lost her parents six months ago and since then she is in a catatonic state. I need help and I am guided to ask, if you could spend few moments with her. My granddaughter's name is Ronja and we live only five minutes away from the store."

The stranger looked into her eyes, suddenly filled with compassion, and replied, "Of course, I would like to see her. It must be divine timing because my whole morning is open. Let me just finish my shopping and then I will meet you at the register again."

Nona could not believe it. She was filled with joy and said, "Thank you so much. This is very unusual for me to be asking a stranger for such a favor."

The woman started laughing and offered Nona her hand, "My name is Sarah."

Nona and Sarah shook hands and Nona said, "My name is Patricia, but most of my friends call me Nona, because I am the nurturing granny mom for all of them."

Both started laughing and Sarah replied, "Well, then I am in good hands, Nona. Nice meeting you."

They finished their shopping and off they went to see Ronja. Nona was excited, her heart was beating strongly and she thanked the Universe for bringing Sarah into her life. She had an "Inner Knowing" that this would shift everything for her grandchild.

As they entered the room, Ronja was lying in bed. The Aide, Louisa, was with her. Nona always referred to Louisa as an angel because she had so much compassion and love for Ronja and all of them. Nona said to her, "Louisa, may I introduce you to Sarah. I invited her to see our beautiful Ronja."

"Welcome Sarah, I am Louisa, and I am the Live in Aide for this family," she said while shaking Sarah's hand. Louisa could not put her finger on it, but something felt very different about this beautiful woman. It almost felt like lots of angels came along with her.

Sarah asked Nona if she was allowed to sit beside Ronja on the bed.

Nona said, "Yes, that would be fine. Would you like us to leave the room?" she asked.

Sarah smiled and said that it was up to them to do whatever felt right. Nona and Louisa decided to stay.

Sarah put her hands together in prayer position and she started speaking a language which they could not understand, *"Manaheta aka. Ehadagodha manaheta aka. Godonaaahate nagoda emanaheta aka."*

Although Nona and Louisa could not perceive the meaning of these words, they could feel it in their hearts. Then Sarah started to sing beautifully in this unfamiliar language. Nona and Louisa decided to close their eyes.

Sarah was speaking in the Cosmic Language of Light, which was a high frequency channeling from the Stars. A language which could not be understood from the linear mind but carried the higher dimensional frequencies of the Cosmos.

Sarah looked at Ronja, who opened her eyes with an empty stare. The woman continued speaking the Language of Light while putting one hand on Ronja's forehead and the other above her navel. She continued to chant for a long time while she moved her hands to different positions on the girl's body. These positions were in the places of the chakra centers in Ronja's body, as well as above her crown and below her feet.

When she was done, Sarah bowed, got up and came towards Nona and Louisa, who had just opened their eyes. Sarah said to them, "Ronja will slowly awaken within the next week. Be patient, as she will need a lot of time to integrate. Your girl travelled far out into the Cosmos to bring in gifts for humankind. She most likely won't remember at the beginning, but she will at the right time. Just trust that. If it is ok with you, I would like to see her once a week for a session. I don't mind coming to your place until she is able to see me at my healing space."

Nona agreed with excitement.

Sarah gave Nona her business card and instructed them to give Ronja additional water through the feeding tube over the next three days. Sarah also impressed upon them the importance of having one of her grandparents or a close friend continuously present at her bedside. It was important for Ronja to see a familiar face when she awoke, so she would have a reference point.

Nona agreed and gave Sarah a big hug. She did not have words to express her gratitude for the blessing which they had just received. Nona truly believed and expected that what Sarah said would come true. That night Nona lit a candle to express her gratitude for being heard.

In the next moment, Ronja opened her eyes and she found herself back in her bedroom, two years after the death of her parents. She joyfully exclaimed, "Oh My God, I am starting to remember!" With these words, she jumped out of bed and went downstairs to have breakfast with Nona.

CHAPTER 2

The Awakening

Ezrael needed to cough while the alarms on the breathing machine were going off. He felt a tube in his throat, air flowing through it out of sync with his own breathing. Then he needed to cough even more and heard a nurse running into his room exclaiming, "Oh my goodness! The boy is up! He is breathing!"

Shortly after, more people appeared in the room. A man in a white coat started talking to him, "Good morning Ezrael, my name is Dr. Bearrow. You are on a breathing machine. I know it is uncomfortable but try to start breathing with the flow of the machine instead of breathing against it. We are going to take the tube out in a moment."

Ezrael saw the nurse administering something into his system through an IV port. He just wanted to reach the tube and take it out himself, but people were holding him down, which made him even more agitated. The medicine made him relax and he could finally breathe with the machine. He saw his blood being drawn. Ezrael wondered, "Where am I? What happened?"

In the next moment, his father, Peter, came running into the room, screaming with joy, "Oh Ezrael! Oh my God! You are awake," he said while making his way through the crowd to his son. Peter hugged Ezrael with tears in his eyes. He smiled as he looked into his son's eyes and said, "Welcome back, son! Welcome back!"

The doctor explained to Peter that they were ready to take his breathing tube out and he would need to wait outside. Peter insisted on staying in the room. They allowed him to stay because the team was aware of all the circumstances.

Ezrael had his mouth suctioned, and a nurse told him what would happen next. Within the next minute the tube was out and he received a facemask, which felt so much more comfortable. They explained that his throat might be sore for a few days and suggested not to rush talking.

Ezrael felt very thirsty and mumbled, "Water!" He promptly received ice chips from the nurse, for which he was very grateful.

As everything settled down, it became quiet. Ezrael started to look around in the room. His father was holding his hand and had his head laying on Ezrael's belly, which felt really good. He saw beautiful colors and prisms everywhere in the room as well as lines going vertical and horizontal in a beautiful, white crystalline color. Then he noticed golden symbols radiating in a round, big ball of light around his father. These sacred geometric symbols appeared to be floating around in a 26-foot round, golden energy structure. He witnessed beautiful colors around his father's body and noticed a tint of black around his head.

Everything in the room vibrated and moved constantly. He had never seen such colors. These colors were interwoven within each other, which created even more new colors. He enjoyed the view because it was so beautiful.

In the next moment, the door opened and his mom, Sarah, came running into the room with tears in her eyes and a big smile. Ezrael was so happy to see her. Sarah crawled on the bed and embraced her son without saying a word. His heart was on his mom's heart. Suddenly, Ezrael felt a lot of energy flowing through his body, which felt so familiar, yet he could not remember when he felt it before.

After she embraced her son, Sarah looked deep into Ezrael's eyes and said, "Welcome back, Ezrael." She was smiling from ear to ear.

Ezrael, still feeling very weak, returned her smile. Sarah took his hand while she moved herself into a chair next to his bed. He saw a beautiful 6-pointed star around each of his parent's bodies. They both had a green color in their heart area. His father's color was closer to a grass green and his mother's was an emerald green color. His mother also had a silver-golden cord, similar to a DNA strand in appearance, which seemed to connect her heart with her third eye. Ezrael was fascinated by his new sight.

Both of his parents were still holding his hands as he was trying to create words, but what came out was hardly audible. His throat felt so sore, yet he was willing to try and all he could whisper was, "What happened?"

His father looked at him and said, "We were hoping that you could explain that to us, because nobody has any idea of what was going on with you, son. Your mother found you and Todd yesterday lying unconscious next to the waterfall and you both were rushed to the hospital. Todd was released on the same day. They kept you overnight and you got worse and worse. None of the doctors knew what was going on with you. They could not find the cause for all of your symptoms and they lost faith in you recovering. It is truly a miracle that you came back!"

Ezrael was exhausted and needed to close his eyes. He could not remember. It felt like too much to think about in this moment.

Slowly Ezrael drifted into a dream state, finding himself somewhere in the Stars. He found himself riding a huge, red dragon. The dragon's name was Goran. He knew this was his dragon. They were surrounded in a big, round, golden light sphere which had three large rings spinning around the outside. There were many symbols floating around in his sphere as well. He recognized two of the sacred geometric symbols; the Ankh and the Infinity Sign.

Everything in the Universe looked so vast. He noticed there was wind and he wondered what was causing it. He also saw his 6-pointed star and many rainbow colors floating in his field. He felt so excited to be experiencing all of this and that it seemed familiar.

Suddenly he heard voices. But where did they come from? Ezrael looked around and from afar he saw a group of people appear. But who were they? The closer they came the more they looked like teenagers of his age. They all were riding dragons, that had the same round sphere surrounding them.

He noticed one girl riding a green dragon in the front of the group and he knew her. It was his beloved friend SumuRa. As they came closer, SumuRa looked at him with a smile and said, "Good work, Lazumar! It took a little bit longer than expected, but you did it!"

Ezrael (Lazumar) smiled back at her and said, "Well, friend, if you guys would have been faster with your work, I could have completed mine sooner!"

Both looked at each other and had to giggle. Finally, he was united again with some of his Star team. His heart was filled with joy as he also greeted his friends Lalunar, Maheta and Merlin. They had been working together in service of the Cosmos since their soul's creation.

Lalunar had shoulder long, red hair and blue eyes. She was riding on a beautiful, orange dragon. Merlin, who had brown hair and light brown eyes, rode on a large, sapphire blue dragon. Maheta, who had long, brown hair and brown eyes, rode on a beautiful, white, majestic dragon.

"Let's go!" SumuRa exclaimed.

Off they went, riding their dragons through the Galaxy. They were on their way to visit Sirius, a beautiful star, which appeared to be a golden-orange color as they approached from afar. As they reached the planet Sirius, they flew to a very specific entry point that not many knew about.

The closer they got to this planet, the more excitement they could feel in their hearts. The dragons knew exactly where they needed to go. When they arrived on the other side of the planet, a beam of light suddenly appeared emanating out from the center of Sirius. The dragons went straight into that beam. As soon as they entered that space, energy started to maneuver them, drawing them closer to the planet. The dragons and the kids were swirling around in the beam of light and everything happened in a fast speed of a second.

In the next moment, they were standing on Sirius. What a beautiful planet it was. It showed many rainbows in the sky. There was crisp, warm and gentle light, but no sun was visible. In the back was a beautiful, majestic crystal tower structure, rising up high in the sky. There were magical waterfalls running in many different directions. All these creeks of the waterfalls ran together, and the interesting part was that the water even ran upstream. Not like on Earth where gravity was experienced.

They walked towards a beautiful, round, crystalline structure. There was a white platform with a golden symbol on it, similar to the flower of life. Suddenly beautiful Cosmic Light Beings appeared. They were around 7 feet tall and made out of light. You could see their human form but they seemed to have a different density, as if you could put your hand right through their bodies. The back of their heads appeared to be elongated.

These beautiful, radiant beings moved to create a circle around them. When the circle was completed, the Cosmic Beings of Light started to hum together. The children could feel the vibration in their bodies.

All of a sudden, the circle opened up and two Light Beings entered. They appeared to be a little taller than the other ones.

They approached each of the children and they greeted each other by the cosmic law; touching their palms and bowing their heads. Then one of the two taller Cosmic Light Beings, Atukar, the male leader, started to speak, *"Mmmmi miii mi mmimimimimmmmimmmmmmmmmmi."*

The children could not understand what he was saying with their minds but in their hearts. They knew he was informing them that it was time for the Transmutation Process.

In the next moment, all of the Cosmic Light Beings standing in the circle, reached out their hands to the side, touching palms while continuing to hum. This created an energy vortex. Suddenly, the golden flower of life structure emanated light energy. The children felt a deep vibration and warmth within their bodies as the energies merged. Then another disk appeared right above them. It was exactly the same structure that was emanating energy from below. The disc above radiated beams of light as well. The energies from above and below merged together with the children. White flickering light birthed out from these light beams and created electric currents that looked like lightning bolts. From these bolts, bright light radiated out and encompassed the whole space. The light became so bright that the children could not see anything else. An explosion of light energy happened within their bodies, light beams shot out from them and into the air. All of a sudden, everything stopped. The disc above was gone, as well as all the different light formations. Now the children looked exactly like the other Cosmic Light Beings, just shorter in size.

Atukar looked at them and said telepathically, "Come!"

They all understood and entered a beautiful, crystalline palace with wide corridors; all felt very pristine and spacious. They entered a beautiful, circular space with crystalline pillars supporting a glass dome ceiling. Above you could see a cobalt blue sky, so clear and appearing as if the sun was shining. However, there was no sun.

The children and the Sirian beings walked towards the center of this space, where there was a very large, round table and many chairs. They all stood around the table and performed the cosmic greeting; hands out to the side, touching each other's palms, bowing their heads. Then they all started to hum and the children did exactly the same as. This was not the first time that the children attended a meeting with the Sirians.

The second taller Light Being, the female leader, Fiandra, started to speak, "Welcome! We will follow protocol and keep this meeting as short as possible because the frequencies are shifting on Earth and we need to get you back as quickly as possible."

Fiandra continued, "You have done great work, Lemurian Star Team. Now more is asked of you. Thanks to Lazumar (Ezrael), the energies have increased and it is time to anchor these powerful energies of divine unconditional love and unity into the Crystalline Grid of the Earth. If these energies cannot be contained properly, it could create chaos on Planet Earth."

Fiandra paused for a moment and continued, "We are helping you to find each other in your human experience on Earth now. Specific instructions are going to get transmitted to you through your Higher Selves. You must follow your internal guidance system in each moment. You will know exactly what to do. Be aware, we cannot interfere with your decisions because you are operating on the planet of free choice. As soon as you go back to Earth, you will not remember any of this. So, we are asking for your permission, now, to send transmissions to you during your dream state?"

All of the children agreed with excitement.

Fiandra, the female Sirian smiled and continued, "As your frequencies and the frequencies on Earth continue to shift, you will attract each other and find the other Lemurians of your Star Team. We will guide you to start light language meditation calls and attend Light Language Ceremonies. These will help you to remember that you are Multidimensional Beings. These higher frequencies of your spoken Language of Light will activate your Quantum DNA further and will uncover your hidden gifts and powers. Once you start to remember, you will know to call us in. Then, we will be able to intervene when you ask. Otherwise, we are not allowed to support the Ascension Process further."

The children nodded their heads filled with excitement.

Next, Atukar said, "Right now, your body is vibrating in our 12th dimensional frequencies, which will activate your DNA further when you are back on Earth. Be aware that the integration of these higher frequencies in your earthly body will cause physical symptoms. It may occur as short-lived tiredness, colds or flu-like states or increased food sensitivities. You will be drawn to more greens and fruits; natural live foods which carry more light. You will automatically prefer to eat organic and natural foods. At the same time, you will stop eating processed foods, because your body will no longer be able to tolerate them."

Atukar continued, "We will send further instruction through the meditation calls when you remember to call us in. It will be important to connect to the Crystalline Grid of Earth, through the Lions Gate and up to the Central Sun and Sirius. You will get guidance how to move forward in divinely, synchronized timing. We are thanking you all for your commitment to Earth and the Cosmos. You have our full support."

Atukar finished with specific instructions for each team member, "SumuRa, you will start working with Tartan, he is a Mountain Being who knows how to connect the crystalline structures throughout the Omniverse. First, you will be trained in how to create energy grids on Earth and then how to interconnect them with your Universe. You will connect to these grids with your heart and will send love out. When you master this skill, you will advance to connecting with all grids throughout the Omniverse. You carry a very unique DNA, a frequency which will automatically activate others around you, who will then start to remember their multidimensional Higher Selves, speak the Language of Light and will know how to use their gifts."

Next, Atukar mentioned to Ezrael, "Lazumar, your main task to focus on right now is to completely remember who you truly are, the Lemurian Master. This is very important because you are carrying DNA codes and energies that allow you to transmute the energies of the dark forces. You are the only one on Earth who carries these specific codes and knows how to use them. Your remembering on how to use these codes is imperative to create peace and balance on Planet Earth. We have given you already the gift of enhanced vision which will help you to navigate yourself and your team through your 3D world."

Atukar continued, "Merlin, you carry specific codes to activate the crystals on Planet Earth. You carry specific remembering in your DNA to create telecommunication grids, which will send and receive information throughout the Omniverse without being detected by the dark forces. You will advance quickly by working with the energy grids. The crystal grids you create will interconnect the earth grids with the frequencies of the Central Sun to realign the Earth with the Cosmos. You will receive initiations into higher levels of your wizardry and you will also work with the powerful Dragon Medicine."

Next, Atukar said, "Maheta, you will work with the Quantum Field and teach your friends first, then the world, how to use imagination for advancement in this field. Your powers and understanding of the Quantum Field are exceptional. You will teach your team how to interact with this field and how to accomplish major advancements for the Earth with ease. You will be the rule breaker. With this purpose you will instill the knowing to your friends, that together you can make the impossible possible. Your endurance and strength will be needed for this work as you will be tested in your human life situations."

Finally, Atukar explained, "Last but not least, Lalunar, you will be the Seer of this group. You are the cracker of the codes and will help the others to successfully complete this mission with your guidance. You will start receiving codes and downloads and will help activate the others as well."

All of the kids seemed very excited about the adventure ahead.

After all instructions were given, Fiandra started to speak, "It is time for you to go back now. The alignment on Earth is happening to get you back safely. We will continue our meeting when it is necessary."

All Sirians and the Lemurian Star Team reached their hands out, side to side again, hummed and bowed. The meeting was now closed. They returned to the platform with the flower of life symbol. The disk appeared above again. The energies emanated from both disks and transformed the children back into their earthly form.

The Star Team said goodbye. The light beam appeared again and catapulted them out into the Cosmos and off they went on their dragons back to Earth.

Ezrael now saw himself back in his hospital bed. He wanted to remember everything he just experienced and wished he could write it down. However, he was so exhausted, closed his eyes and fell asleep for 24 hours.

After he awoke, the hospital staff ran some tests on him. All the test results came back normal. Ezrael and his parents felt relieved. The doctors wanted to observe Ezrael at least for one more night, but he insisted on going home. So, they reluctantly released him. Ezrael felt so much stronger after his long sleep. He felt like he was born anew. Ezrael was excited about going home and he knew his life would never be the same. His parents packed his belongings and off they went home, with a feeling of adventure in the air.

CHAPTER 3

The Meeting of the Lemurian Council of the Cosmic Heart & Light

Imero, the Emperor of Darkness on Planet Earth and Ammagant, his disciple, were in Imero's study. Since their defeat, no words had been spoken. They had been defeated after 2000 years of ruling Earth. The air was filled with tension and the silence was felt with intensity.

Imero paced up and down in his study, deep in thought, and finally spoke, "We have been defeated and I am still perplexed about how this could have happened. The 'emerald green, pure, love energy' has been spread over the entire Earth. At this moment, even though it is only on the surface of the Earth, I know it will soon penetrate into Inner Earth and then into the Cosmos." Imero felt so disgusted just by thinking of this 'love energy'.

Ammagant replied, "Imero, it might be time that we call in the dark forces of Inner Earth and send an SOS out to 'the Gedoha Clan'; the dark forces of all the different star systems. I am aware that you are the Emperor of Darkness on Earth, and I do not question for a moment your power or authority."

Ammagant paused for a moment and then continued, "The only reason we were defeated was because they had help from the unseen, benevolent forces, which we were not aware of. We need to act soon! More and more humans are getting infused with this green vibration, which will make their hearts more open and will break them free of mind control sooner than later. You know, Master, the only way we can keep them continuously influenced with our dark energies is through mind control. When love takes over fear, we can't influence them anymore."

Imero replied in a stern voice, "You are right, Ammagant. We do not have any time to waste. Set up a private meeting with the Inner Earth People and with our friends from 'the Gedoha Clan'. Make sure it will be a secret meeting. Nobody else can find out, otherwise we will be disempowered immediately. Go now, Ammagant! No time to waste!"

Ammagant put on his invisibility cloak, went to the door and off he traveled through the vast space.

Master Merlin, the white wizard, and Novix, his disciple from the elf clan, sat around a fire smiling. Both were Ezrael's Guides in the spirit world.

Novix said, "Merlin, this 'emerald green, pure love energy' is so healing for the planet. What a beautiful gift. Now everything will change for the better of humanity. You did good work, Merlin!"

Novix and Merlin enjoyed feeling these new energies also entering their hearts.

Merlin replied, "Thank you, Novix, for your kind words. Yes, a big shift has occurred on Earth. One which nobody had expected to happen so fast. To think that a short time ago it was a strong possibility that humanity would destroy themselves again."

"Well, the fifth time is the charm! As you know, Merlin, five is the number for change and this fifth civilization has finally changed the course for the humans and Earth," Novix replied.

Merlin said, "Yes, Novix. But it is not over yet. The Ascension Process, as you know, always goes through a period of darkness before the light will shine through fully. I have complete knowing that this 'emerald green love energy' has changed the vibration in people's hearts. I see all the highest potentials for humanity. How beautiful it will be when we step into the era of peace on this planet. I can't wait to witness the full DNA activation which will make humans find God within themselves. What wonders are in store when all beings are starting to collaborate and to access their multidimensional powers," Merlin replied.

"Yes, Master, it will be beautiful!" Novix stated joyfully.

Merlin continued, "For now they have to go through the processes of DNA activations and transmutations. These new energies will help the unawakened humans to free themselves from the Matrix of mind control. It won't be easy, sometimes uncomfortable and unfortunately we can only hold space for now."

"Can't we do something to help them in this process? Why can't we just take their implants out and make them free?" Novix asked.

Merlin answered, "Remember the Earth is the planet of free choice. We have to be careful not to intervene without invitation. They need to become aware of their own Divinity and Us first. Then we can support them on an individual basis as they ask for help. You know, this is a perfect grand plan."

After a short pause, Merlin said, "Novix, let us go! It is time for our council meeting."

In the next moment, both of them vanished. Where did they go?

Instantly, Merlin and Novix were seated at a large, round table. They arrived at the Lemurian Council Meeting of the Cosmic Heart & Light. There were many familiar faces as well as a number of new and interesting looking Light Beings already present.

Atukar and Fiandra, the representatives from Sirius, had joined the meeting. Dhalia and Okonis, were representing the Pleiadian Star System. ChabA and Thalum, dwarf like in appearance, were the Arcturian representatives. Imukah, from the Central Sun, showed his face as well for this important council meeting.

There was a funny looking large, white Elephant Being who stood out like a sore thumb. His name was Buddha Ganesh, the mayor and representative of Inner Earth. He was well respected by his comrades for his dedication and tireless work of transmuting and amplifying energies for the Earth to foster peace.

Merlin and Novix represented Earth in this intergalactic council meeting.

One of the Sirians, Fiandra, started to talk, "Thank you all for joining our meeting. Let us open our Lemurian Council Meeting of the Cosmic Heart & Light."

They held hands and toned, *"AAAAHHHHHHHHHHHMMMMMMMM,"* several times which unified their energies together. It was beautiful.

Anukah, the Sirian male representative, spoke with intensity, "Welcome everyone! "Phase 2" has been established much faster than expected, by the surprisingly good work of the humans. Merlin, your work was magical and we have been observing you from afar. You have chosen the right children for this task. Good work with all of them. As "Phase 2" has been integrated, we are now able to support Earth more through the higher frequencies. We will initiate further DNA activations."

"Yes! Thank you!" Merlin replied and asked, "What do you suggest, Imukah? What are the next frequency transmissions that will help to awaken the people on Planet Earth even more?"

Imukah responded, "Well, as calculated earlier and keeping everything in synchronistic order, the next two time capsules will be opened during Summer Solstice. These time capsules will activate codes of remembering and increase compassion on Planet Earth. The next phase of transmission will continue right after the Summer Solstice during the Solar Eclipse. During the eclipse time, I will send down transmissions through the Lions Gate Portal. I have already started coding the transmissions. It will be something that has never been possible before this moment in time, which is very exciting and will help the Earthlings to evolve faster."

Dhalia, the female Pleiadian asked, "I thought the transmissions were not able to be sent out to Earth yet, because the humans are not ready? This is what we discussed in our last meeting."

"Well, by surprise, Dhalia," Imukah responded, "the humans are waking up pretty fast. The group of children, Merlin specifically chose because of their Pleiadian DNA structure, are already doing intense work. We have not seen anything like this before on the other planets who went through their Ascension. These kids are superheroes, as you would say."

Anukah joined the discussion, "As you all know, the children, or the Lemurian Star Team, as we fondly call them, have visited with us. They have received the codes and the new implants for the downloads. They will need these energies for the Solstice and Solar Eclipse transmissions to help them remember how to use their powers even further."

"It seems like everything is on track," Merlin stated contently.

Anukah continued, "Alright then, we will proceed with the plan. The two time capsules will open during Solstice and then during the Solar Eclipse you will send down the transmissions. Let's make sure the Earth is protected during the full dark period of the Solar Eclipse. As you know, during these few minutes, dark frequencies can come in to counteract."

Imukah replied, "No worries, Anukah. I have it all calculated and I am sending additional frequency codes to Earth for those who already have an activated heart."

"Alright, so we are on track," Anukah replied. "What is the update on the Pleiadian group activation support system?"

Dhalia responded, "We have started working with a group of influential scientists about economic restructuring in preparation for the upcoming planetary energy shift to integrity, assuming the Star Team nails their mission."

Dhalia continued, "We received permission from many to work with them during their dream states, downloading information regarding new paradigms for the political, social, economic and educational systems. We are also guiding them with messages on how to reunite with the other members of their soul groups. We are beyond on track. We have never seen anything like this before. It is quite a surprise and it is showing us that the DNA structures we have chosen for the Earth Beings were the right ones. Adding the additional Pleiadian DNA strand made all the difference."

"I have to agree, Dhalia," Merlin added with a smile.

The male Arcturian, Thalum, asked in a very sharp, metallic voice, "What are we going to do about the uniting of the dark forces of Inner Earth and 'the Gedoha Clan'? We are all aware that this meeting is taking place as we speak."

Buddha Ganesh, Mayor of Inner Earth, started to speak, "The Reptilians are going to revolt, as we would expect. We gave them a choice. Either they can surrender with honor and be rehabilitated with love or they will be forced to go to the Central Sun for life review and sentencing. Many have already surrendered! Some continue to conspire against the light forces with the Cabal people on Earth, who have free choice as well."

Thalum continued, "When the *'love frequency'* on Planet Earth rises to a certain point, they will no longer have the choice to voluntarily leave. At this point we are watching."

"We are aware that Imero and Ammagant will reach out to the Martians and the Malbecians, who are part of 'the Gedoha Clan'," Thalum continued, "as well as other betrayal parties from other star systems. We are observing the dark forces and transmuting as many energies as possible. It is no surprise that Occuna, the Dark Emperor of the Galaxies, cannot be traced. I know he will be found where the dark forces meet. I will watch out and keep everyone informed."

"Yes, this is important," Anukah continued. "Thank you all for joining our meeting. You all shall report to me and we will schedule our next meeting when appropriate."

For closing the meeting, all of them touched palms around the circle, closed their eyes, bowed their heads and disappeared in a flash of light.

CHAPTER 4

The Quantum Field

Ronja got dressed, went downstairs and fell into the arms of her loving grandmother with a big smile on her face. After the embrace, Nona looked at Ronja and said, "Dear child, you are quite cheerful today. This is so wonderful to see!"

"Yes, Nona," Ronja replied, "I am starting to remember. I just had many visions and observed everything that happened to all of us after the accident. Even though I was in the coma, I witnessed everything from above. I saw you praying to God outside for help. I also saw you meeting Sarah at the store that day when you were looking for incense. Did this really happen?"

Nona stared at her granddaughter in amazement and replied, "Yes, it did happen! Oh, my heavens! How is this possible?"

Ronja was excited about the confirmation she just received from her grandmother. She replied, "I don't know how, Nona, but I do know something big is unfolding and I feel excited about what is to come."

Ronja paused for a moment and continued, "Although some of the visions I witnessed were very sad. I was made aware of how hard it was for you and grandpa to take care of me, while dealing with your own loss. I want to thank you for all that you have done for me, Nona. Without you, I would not have made it through."

Nona, still a little stunned by the accuracy of Ronja's visions, smiled and said, "Thank you my love. I did the best I could. I know deep in my heart that you waking up was a miracle and it would not have been possible without divine intervention. Anything else you want to share about what you saw?"

"Yes, Nona," Ronja continued, "I am glad you asked. I saw myself traveling through the Cosmos with my large, green dragon, Elmuthan. This might sound strange, however, it felt like I have done this many times before and it was like I was "home". I am not sure if this was all just a dream, but Nona, it feels very real and true to me."

Nona started smiling and said, "It seems like you are starting to remember something important. If I recall correctly, Sarah mentioned that this was going to happen. Maybe it is time for you to talk with Sarah again."

"Yes, Nona, I was thinking the same thing," Ronja replied as she sat down at the breakfast table and ate her oatmeal, which Nona prepared for her. Ronja continued, "I have not seen her for over a year now."

"Yes, Ronja. Time flies," Nona replied.

After breakfast, Ronja decided to go for a walk to visit the waterfall, which was close to her house. It was her sacred space; her favorite place to meditate and contemplate. Ronja asked Nona for some corn meal to make offerings to the land. She filled up her water bottle, put her cell phone in her pocket and off she went.

During the walk, she felt a heaviness in her chest while deep in thought. Ronja was remembering all that had happened to her over the past six months since she woke up. Her body had been so weak and it took time for her to get strong again. The daily physical therapy was sometimes very painful because she had lost all her muscle mass. She endured the slow recovery with the help of Sarah and many other caring people. Ronja also struggled through many emotional battles during this time. She felt abandoned by God because of what had happened to her. How could something so terrifying be allowed to happen to anyone.

Ronja needed intensive psychological counseling sessions to help her deal with the grief and shock of her parents' death. Ronja also saw Sarah on a regular basis. During their last session, while Sarah spoke in the Cosmic Language of Light, Ronja cried for the first time in six months. It had all been buried inside of her so deeply. Once she cracked the deep wound open, it could finally heal. Yes, Ronja remembered that day. They both knew, their work together was done for now. At the end of this session, they hugged each other.

After the embrace, Sarah looked sternly into Ronja's eyes and said, "You have done well, Ronja. I am very proud of you. Now it is time for you to find out, who you truly are. This is your path to take on your own, my love. Nobody can do this for you. If you are willing to look inside of yourself and endure, you will find all the treasures."

Ronja replied, "Thank you, Sarah, for all you have done for me. I truly appreciate it. I know what I have to do now."

Sarah smiled at her and said, *"Gonaheta aka. Nedumis agara onahetaka!"*

Ronja was surprised when she heard herself reply in the Cosmic Language of Light for the first time, "Ekta chorga. Nanahata ejamaka."

Ronja did not understand what she just said, but she was more excited than ever knowing that she had tapped into something new. She finally started speaking the Cosmic Language of Light herself!

Both laughed out loud full of joy, while they embraced each other again.

"It is all unfolding in divine time, Ronja," Sarah said, "just follow your heart and you will always be at the right place at the right time. Staying in the 'NOW' is all you need. So be present and aware. This is how you will experience the magic of the Universe and how it interacts with you in every moment. Trust, ask, expect and you shall receive. I know we will see each other again when the time is right."

These were the last words Sarah had spoken to her over a year ago. Ronja had contemplated contacting Sarah many times, but something inside of her made her feel, that it was not the right time yet. Today felt different.

Ronja remembered going to the waterfall after their last meeting. She recalled sitting down underneath her favorite tree, giving offerings to Mother Gaia, closing her eyes to meditate and the amazing vision that followed that day.

Through her mind's eye, Ronja saw very tall, beautiful Light Beings surrounding her in a circle. She could feel their presence.

A gentle breeze stroked Ronja's cheeks. She saw, through her mind's eye, the Cosmic Light Beings holding up their hands and touching palms around the circle. In the next moment, she saw a beautiful, emerald green colored energy flowing from their hearts into her heart. It felt so warm and soothing. The girl felt heat in the palms of her hands and soles of her feet.

Next, she saw a golden color emanating from the Cosmic Light Beings and merging with the emerald green in her heart. In that moment, something magical happened.

Ronja felt for the first time being ONE with all there is. She found God within herself which made her cry. She felt like she was "home"; the Love of the Creator and Mother Gaia within her being. This feeling state she experienced was called "Grace". Ronja knew this KNOWING of God within her was sacred and no one could ever take this away from her. She stayed in meditation for quite some time, tears flowing from her eyes. This time it was out of joy and not out of sorrow.

As quickly as the Cosmic Light Beings appeared, they disappeared. Little did she know at this time, that she had been visited by her Sirian friends.

Ronja remembered opening her eyes after the vision and felt deep gratitude for what she had experienced. She looked at the sun and the sky with a smile.

From that day on, Ronja carried a spark in her eyes. She felt so much Divine Love within herself and was so thankful to be alive. Joyfully she sang Light Language out into the world. Even though she could not understand what it meant at that time, it felt good and that was most important.

Yes, Ronja now recalled this life changing event that happened over a year ago, as she made way to the waterfall. Since then, she spoke Light Language daily and her abilities expanded. Sometimes she could understand what she was saying through her heart. She wished for friends in her life who shared the same gifts. She felt alone in all of this, which made her sad from time to time.

Ronja still wondered sometimes, about these Cosmic Light Beings. She had not seen them since, although she continued to visit and meditate at the waterfall. She never told anyone about this sacred experience, which had changed Ronja forever. Her friends and family often commented on her newly expressed joyful spirit.

When she reached the waterfall, she sat down under her favorite tree and gave her offerings to Mother Gaia. She closed her eyes and envisioned a grounding cord from her navel dropping down into the Crystalline Grid of the Earth. And she was grounded to Earth, grounded to Earth, grounded to Earth. Next, she took deep breaths and focused on expanding her heart field by feeling Divine Love within her. She experienced pure unconditional love and compassion for herself.

Every time she did this, it was like magic. She activated a magnetic field in which all energies were drawn to her through the feeling of Love. She felt all the boundaries of her body distinctly and attracted multiple forms of energy into her heart which flowed through her entire body. Although she was not aware of it at the time, she was actively working with the Quantum Field in a very focused manner.

Each meditation was a little different. Sometimes she saw herself sitting in a beautiful, golden structure with three golden rings surrounding her. As she meditated these rings started to turn into different directions. It almost felt like she could hear a sound in the stillness of them turning. She often saw many geometric symbols and numbers floating around in this space, especially around the outside of the sphere.

She loved being in this space. She knew that the shifting and combining of the symbols and number sequences created an unlocking of codes. This attracted others who she was destined to meet. When she was done with the meditation, Ronja gave thanks for the blessings she had received, grounding herself in the here and now with deep breathing. As she walked out of the woods she decided to call Sarah.

When she got back to cell connection, she was surprised to see that Sarah had actually texted her while she had been meditating at the waterfall. Ronja got goosebumps as she read the text from

Sarah, "Dear Ronja, it is time that you meet my son, Ezrael. I trust it will help you both to meet. We are home now and looking forward to seeing you as soon as possible. With love and light! Sarah! Enagoda mataka!"

Ronja loved when these synchronicities happened because it reassured her that she was in the flow of total alignment with the Universe. She texted Sarah back that she was on her way and excited to meet her son. Ronja's heart was pounding nervously. The walk to Sarah's house felt endless.

CHAPTER 5

The Inner Earth Meeting

Ammagant had returned to Imero's study and had arranged a meeting. Yes, Imero was hopeful that a collaboration with other dark forces, who will support his mission, will bring down the light. He was still grieving the old paradigm, his kingdom, which he controlled for thousands of years. With sadness, he looked back at how he loved watching the humans fight and kept them controlled in the Matrix. He had received energy from their fear and anger. He felt weak at the moment, but thankfully his energies are still existing on the planet. Not everything has been destroyed yet, and he had hope that with the help of Galactic and Inner Earth Beings, he could get all his power back.

The Matrix was an energy structure, which has been opposed to Earth by free choice through Imero. He was the grand creator of a simulation machine, which created illusions on Planet Earth. It made the humans forget their power, their God Source, and kept them in mind control.

The Matrix was an energetic structure in which Imero sent out frequencies and made humans believe whatever he wanted. It was the best game Imero had ever created. Few people got out of the Matrix in these years. The two results were: not being listened to or being eradicated. Their multidimensional remembering and using their powers did not have much impact on Earth. Imero's system was an over and over repeating energy circuit, which ran like an autopilot system, and continuously gave Imero power through the human's fear states.

Because of this unexpected and sudden energy shift on the Planet, his program was not running properly anymore. More and more people started to wake up to their own divine self-love, integrity, and compassion. Their level of consciousness got raised and through free will, they freed themselves from the Matrix of mind control. The Matrix has failed and something new needed to be established, but Imero was not yet sure what it would be.

"Imero, it is time for the meeting! The dark forces are ready to meet us," Ammagant said.

"Yes, let us go. We do not want to be late," Imero replied.

They walked outside, entered a doorway next to the study, which almost looked like a large rabbit hole. As soon as they entered, they were in a fast speed elevator getting transported into Inner Earth, to a secret place that not many knew about.

As they reached their destination, they exited the transport station and found themselves in a beautiful hallway. Who would have thought that there was light in Inner Earth but yet, there was. It almost looked like the outside of the planet, but the structures seemed simpler and more in resonance with the Earth.

Ammagant and Imero were greeted by a crocodile looking creature. This was an Inner Earth Being, which has lived in Inner Earth for quite some time. There species was called "Reptors or Reptilians", and looked like larger crocodiles walking on two feet who received energies from the humans through fear states as well.

The Reptor's name was Kamit, he was the disciple of the King and Queen of the Reptilians. Kamit was responsible for finding and maintaining habitats for the Reptors and was overseeing their battery charging station.

Imero and Ammagant followed him into a great hall, where several different people had already gathered around a table.

One of them was a Martian named Kedrek, who looked like the Mars figures you would see in cartoons. The Martian was very tall and slim. His ears looked like round, long flutes. Kedrek was brownish-green in color and its fingers were very long and thin, as well as the toes on the feet. Interestingly enough, it appeared that this creature only had four toes and fingers to count on each side. He and his group lived in the Inner Planet of Mars, which not many knew about.

A humanoid looking small person was presented as well. Her name was Ledura. She was representing the Malbecians. She looked like an old woman very much in human form, shorter in size though.

The last Inner Earth clan member, who was at the table, was an Insectoid. It was an ant-like looking creature, Hedoha was her name.

After everyone had gathered around the table, Kamit the Reptilian, started to speak, "Thank you all for coming to this important gathering today. As you are all aware, the humans have changed the plan by surprise. They have increased the energy on Earth, which makes it very uncomfortable for us to live here. On Planet Earth the frequencies are continuing to increase which make us worry. We might need to look for another home, as the energies become intolerable living conditions for us. Also, our fear battery charging station had a decrease of 30% since the last big energy shift. This '*love energy*' is not good for us."

Kamit, the Reptilian, continued, "I would like to get a report from each species today and want to work on a plan on what to do next."

Hedoha, the ant-like looking creature started to speak, "Our clan is very excited about the changes on Planet Earth. Our Master and Mastress have started working with the Earthlings a long time ago and they made agreements to help each other with resources and technology. We are not affected by the changes on Earth."

"Thank you, Hedoha, for speaking," Kamit continued and asked, "Do you still have your small group on your side, who will help us with the Interference?" Kamit asked.

"Yes, Master, we are all ready whenever you are!" Hedoha replied.

"What is the update on the Martians?" Kamit asked.

Kedrek, the male Martian responded, "We are quite upset about what is happening on Earth. We have increased our frequency transmissions of anger and hate. Although the love vibration is still higher, we think that we will catch up soon. There is nothing to worry about, yet. We still have it under control. Imero's Matrix is still working efficiently enough."

"Thank you, Kedrek. I am pleased to hear that," Kamit replied.

"How about the Malbecians. What is your report?" Kamit asked.

Ledura, the Malbecian, started to speak in a very metallic voice, "Thank you for inviting us to this meeting and thank you for being for the same cause as us. We are not worried about this little increase. Yes, it was a shift but as we know from the past, the humans still destroyed themselves from civilization to civilization. We have full confidence that this will continue again. The humans are still stuck on a hamster wheel and continue to pollute the planet and create wars. Nothing has changed besides this little green energy."

"This is good to hear," Imero said, "I have quite some concerns about that, because these *'love energies'* spread so fast. The biggest problem in my perspective is, that this high energy helps the Lemurians to remember."

"Why are you bringing up the Lemurians? We have not heard and detected them for thousands of years, Imero!" Kamit asked.

"As you might know, Kamit," Imero continued. "The high Civilizations of Lemuria had worked on DNA activations and had telepathic properties. They were such a heart centered culture and had included all star systems, which brought all the ancient teachings from the Stars to this planet. They carried unity consciousness in the most sacred ways. I am concerned that this emerald green color with gold and silver combinations will make the Lemurians remember."

After being deep in thought for a moment, Imero continued, "We can't underestimate the Lemurians this time. They have knowledge of all star systems in their DNA and if they wake up, they will be instantly starting to remember, get out of the Matrix and start uniting. Their unity consciousness is unfortunately for us very incredible. These Lemurians are all critical thinkers and leaders. We have never seen 'leader's DNA' like this one anywhere else in the Galaxy," Imero said.

Ammagant stated, "I have witnessed them meeting already. It almost seems like a magnetic force is uniting them together. They must have worked on that during their Lemurian time, because these energies are unstoppable, and it seems, that they help each other to remember, by just getting connected with each other. Do not forget they were experts in the Quantum Field."

Ammagant paused for a moment and then continued, "This is of great concern, especially as many of them are parents of Crystal Children and Starseeds. With their upgrade in their DNA structure, they will automatically activate their children, and this is the concern. When the children get activated, we will have no more control over them."

The Marsian responded, "Yes, you are right Ammagant, but the amount of them is very small. There is nothing to worry about!"

"We have underestimated the humans before," Imero responded sternly. "This is of great concern at the moment and I do not want us to take this lightly. Especially if the humans transmute into the Monsters of Lemuria!"

"Yes, of course," the Martian replied, "We will continue to send interference transmission to Earth, in a way that we are not getting detected from intergalactic federations."

After a short period of silence, Kamit looked at Imero and said, "...And there is something Imero, you will need to do!"

"What is it?" Imero asked.

"We asked Occuna for help, the Emperor of Darkness of the Galaxies. He has high mind control technology and we have asked him to help us with the existing Earth problem. Occuna felt this uncomfortable Earth shift as well. He will visit you soon and might ask for a trade. Whatever he wants for his help on Earth, please consider it, Imero," the Reptilian stated.

"I will talk to him, but he needs to understand that I am the Emperor of the Dark Forces here on Earth," Imero stated proudly.

"Yes, we do understand," Kamit replied, "but for now we need to work together."

Although Imero agreed, he wished he could have the power all to himself and for himself.

Kamit continued, "Thank you all for joining today. It was a very productive meeting. Everyone keeps me updated continuously. I want to get reports about transmissions, meetings, plans, interference, everything immediately! Is that clear to all of you?" Kamit asked.

All of the members agreed, gave their goodbyes and left the meeting room.

Imero and Ammagant exited the same way as they entered and returned to their interdimensional home, which did not exist in physical matter on Earth but in an energetic structure which could be felt, heard and seen. It was deep inside the Shastian Mountain, a very Lemurian place. They picked this location as a home, because they knew that no one would ever expect them to live with their enemies. So far they have not been detected.

Back in Imero's study, Ammagant said, "This was a very good meeting, Master. I will continue to watch over the Lemurians as I am still connected with Todd, the Chosen One's friend. Because of this connection, I will know as soon as they meet again and will give you report."

"Yes, that sounds perfect. Thank you, Ammagant," Imero responded. "It all seems very promising."

Both of them were hopeful and Imero was looking forward to finally meeting the Emperor of Darkness of the Galaxies.

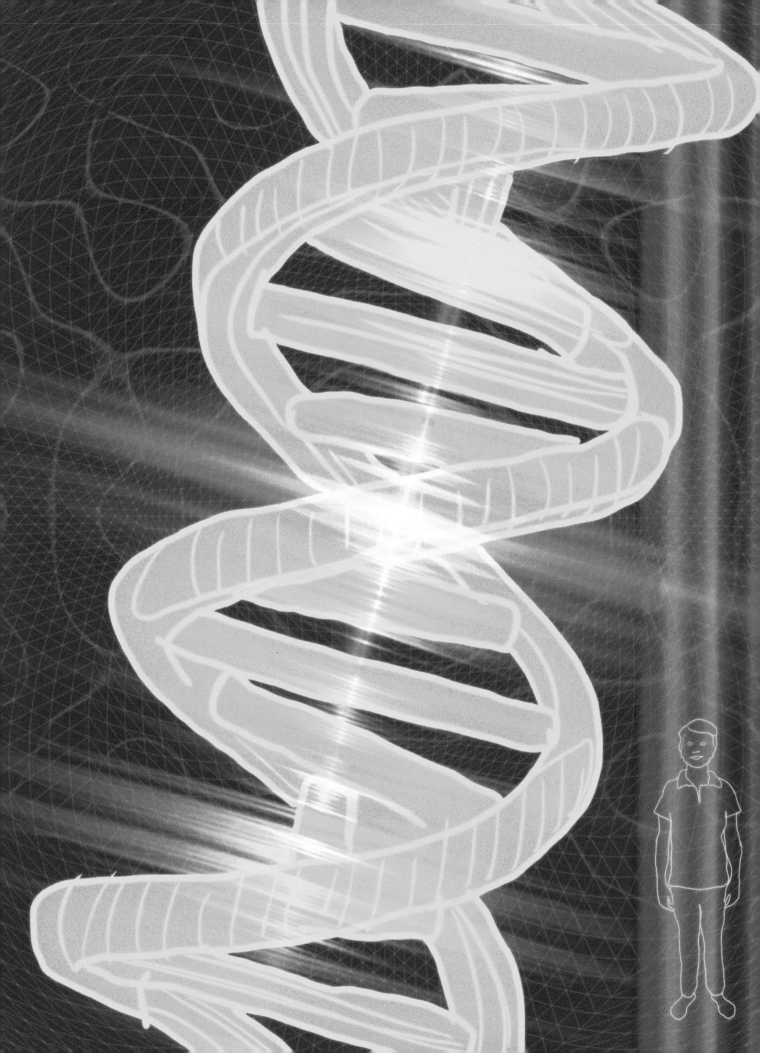

CHAPTER 6

The First Encounter

When Ezrael returned home after staying in the hospital for two nights, he had a bowl of vegetable soup and decided to rest on the couch in the living room. He was glad his parents brought him home today. Ezrael was still amazed by what he could see since his awakening in the hospital. Everything seemed to have an energy field around it. He could still see the auric field of his parents and it was fun for him to watch, when two people's energy fields merged together. He could intuitively pick up some feeling states related to these colors as they merged.

His mom came into the living room and asked how he was doing. He told her that he felt stronger and very peaceful. Then he said, "I also feel lighter and quite happy, considering I almost died." He was not sure if it was the time to share more about his new ability yet.

Sarah smiled, sat next to him on the couch and said, "You really scared us. Thank God I found you when I did. I wish you had listened to me and waited until after the ceremony, which was planned for the morning you left. The journey you attempted was very dangerous!"

Ezrael apologized and explained, "I saw your note about not leaving the house and did not think it was a big deal to just meet Todd for a quick breakfast at the waterfall. I did not know about a ceremony. What was the ceremony for?"

Sarah replied, "The ceremony was to be an activation and initiation but it seems like you did it in your own ways." Sarah had to grin on her face when saying that.

Ezrael said with a puzzled expression, "Mom, it seems like you know more then you are telling me."

Ezrael felt a little annoyed. His mom always spoke in mysterious ways which he often did not get at all. But this time, Ezrael did not give in and said to Sarah, "It is time for you to explain more. After this experience, I deserve to hear it all!"

Sarah replied, "My words might not make sense to you in this moment, but they will when the time is right." Suddenly, Sarah felt a flush of energy flowing through her and started to speak in the Cosmic Language of Light and its translation to Ezrael,

"Godaeha anagaka dehamaga dodaeha eta goda nata madaka!"

"You are on your Path of Awakening!"

"Nedaahada goda badadoda edahada ga gostaheda nodageta ha!"

"The first Initiation has been successfully completed by you."

"Madagoda ehadaka detaoda madagora edagahadeta madaka!"

"Trust your new friends, who are coming into your life soon and let them help you remember!"

"Adageda godohata edamadagotaka. Adorada menagoda ehadatakadahe!"

"Your remembering will reveal your gifts and how to use them for humankind!"

Ezrael felt intense energy flowing through his body, while he received her message. He did not know what to say at the moment.

Sarah continued after a long pause of silence in a soft voice, "Speaking of new friends: do you remember the story I told you about the girl, Ronja, who was in a catatonic state for six months? She went through a similar experience as you. Do you remember that?"

"Yes, Mom. I do. You never introduced me to her, although you said you would," Ezrael replied.

"Well," Sarah said, "the time was not right yet. You both had to do your own work first. But the time is now. I invited her over today to meet you and she will be here soon. If that's ok with you, of course."

Ezrael said excitedly, "Of course! I guess you knew I would say "yes" since she is already on her way here," he laughed. "I am happy to talk with someone who has experienced something similar to what I just did. Maybe she will help me to make sense of it all. When is she coming?" Ezrael asked.

"Probably soon," Sarah replied.

"Alright," Ezrael said, "and there is one more thing weighing on my mind that I would like to talk to you about." Ezrael really wanted to see his best friend Todd. He was hesitant and curious, because he knew that Todd had something to do with his hospitalization.

With this thought in his mind, he said to his mom, "I would like to have a meeting with Todd and I want you to be there. Something happened at the waterfall that day because of him and I want to find out more about it. The last things I remember were falling into the grass in pain right after Todd appeared at the waterfall. His energy felt dark and he acted very strangely. The closer he came the worse I felt. He even said his name was Imero, the Emperor of Darkness, and wanted me to look into his eyes. I did look into his eyes and I do not remember anything after that."

"I agree, Ezrael," Sarah said. "It is important to talk with Todd but let us give it some time. I am going to text him to reach out to me instead of you for now, until you feel better. How does that sound? We will know when it's the right time to meet Todd."

"Yes, thank you, Mom! This all sounds good," he said with a tired sigh. Ezrael rested his head on the couch and said, "I am going to rest now until Ronja comes." He felt tired and closed his eyes for a few minutes. Sarah left the room to let him rest.

In the past, he often felt a little annoyed with his mom when she answered like this. She always seemed to talk about the right time and divine timing. Now, she left things open again, but for the first time he started to understand where she was coming from. He trusted her knowing, it resonated with his own.

A half hour later, Sarah greeted Ronja at her front door. They hugged each other and laughed. Ronja was so excited to be seeing Sarah again.

"Oh Ronja, it is so good to see you. I have to say that I really missed you. I stayed in contact with Nona and she said you are doing well," Sarah said.

"Yes, Sarah, I am well and I was just thinking of you earlier this week because something has been shifting lately. I am starting to have visions that feel very familiar to me. I believe I am starting to remember more of what happened when I was in the coma," Ronja replied.

"Are you willing to share? I would love to hear your revelations!" Sarah replied.

"I am starting to remember the Cosmos. I know now, that I am a Starseed, and I am not originally from this planet. I have traveled through space and have connected during meditation with tall Cosmic Light Beings. I received so much love. I can actually feel like I have found God within me. I am not sure if this makes any sense to you, Sarah," Ronja explained.

"Yes, it all makes sense to me, "Sarah replied and suddenly started speaking in the Language of Language, *"Gonoheta aka magonimi delo adaheta aka!"*

Ronja felt the vibration in her heart and replied, *"Yetaheja, omanota behagata olagena gabaka."*

Both started laughing and hugged each other again.

After the embrace Sarah said, "Let me see if Ezrael is ready to see you. He just got out of the hospital today."

"What happened?" Ronja asked.

"We do not really know, yet. He went through a similar experience like you, Ronja. In his case it all happened very fast over the last two days. He went to the ICU and nobody could tell us what was going on with him. We almost lost him, Ronja. We just got back today and he is resting. It is important to make this first meeting short but it felt urgent to get you two together as soon as possible," Sarah explained.

Ronja agreed and Sarah went into the living room to check on her son to see if he was ready to meet her and he was. Sarah brought Ronja in to meet Ezrael.

As soon as Ronja saw him, she could not believe her eyes, as he was the boy from her dreams. The one who just won over the dark. Ronja was so surprised that she could not say a word and could not even shake his hand.

He looked at Ronja and said, "You look like you just saw a ghost. But don't worry I do not bite," he said with a grin on his face. Somehow, she felt familiar to him.

Ronja still could not say anything. Sarah thankfully said, "Ezrael, this is Ronja. Ronja this is Ezrael."

"Nice to meet you, Ezrael," she said as she could finally find her voice again.

"Same here," he said, while thinking that she was reacting a little weird. "Oh well," he thought, "thank God I am used to weird. I am used to it from living with my Mom."

"Ronja, would you like anything to drink?" Sarah asked.

"Some water would be great, thank you," Ronja replied with a nervous smile.

Sarah left the room and both of them were quiet for a while until Ronja asked, "What happened to you?"

Ezrael felt very comfortable around Ronja, as if he knew her already. So, he told her everything he remembered.

When Sarah reentered the room with a glass of water, Ezrael asked his mom, "Why did you want to hold ceremony with me, Mom?"

Sarah gave Ronja the water and replied, "Ceremonies are sacred rituals, which help us align with the unseen, benevolent forces to activate our gifts, our DNA. We honor Mother Gaia and our Ancestors, which supports our alignment and awakening process. I felt you needed it for your journey."

"But what is my journey, Mom?" Ezrael felt irritated by not knowing.

"All of us are on a journey to remember who we truly are. When we find God within us, open our hearts to self-love and compassion, we open up to energies that give us access to powers we have never dreamed of. We are then able to co-create 'Heaven on Earth'. This is the magic," Sarah replied.

After a few moments of deep silence, she continued, "We all are powerful. We all are gifted and unique. It is our choice to evolve and fulfill our mission to support the Ascension of humanity. Awakened souls are here to help others to awaken, to remember their multidimensional Higher Selves and to unite. We can't do it alone."

"Are you telling me that we are all 'the Chosen Ones'?" Ezrael asked.

"Yes! We are all unique and powerful beyond our minds comprehension. We just have to follow the guidance of Spirit with an open heart. We all carry activation codes and we have chosen to be here during this exciting time to support each other evolve through DNA activations."

"What does DNA activation mean, Sarah?" Ronja asked.

Sarah replied, "We carry a very specific blueprint in our DNA. Many believe that we carry other Star being's DNA, including a very specific strand of Pleiadian DNA within us. With the increase of frequencies on the planet and through specific planetary events, our DNA has started to vibrate on a higher frequency which causes the DNA strands to perform on a higher level. Not much has been explored yet about the DNA being Quantum. It is my belief that the Quantum Field provides the magic that makes it all happen."

After a short pause, Sarah continued, "We are living in exciting times like never before. Our souls have experienced thousands of lives on this planet and other planetary systems. Our souls have worked hard to raise consciousness on Earth. In many lifetimes, we did not experience happy endings. Nevertheless, we kept coming back because we knew what was possible. We are finally in this magical time where for the first time everything can shift for the better. We can finally access energies we have only dreamed of. As we learn to continually access the Quantum Field, where there is no time, we can release all Karma instantly and finally be free. As we calibrate on a higher frequency, we are able to remember and tap into our cosmic, multidimensional Higher Selves. When we enter the space of Quantum with a compassionate and unconditional heart, the Matrix becomes the old paradigm!"

"Can you tell us about what you have remembered so far, Sarah?" Ronja asked curiously.

Sarah explained, "Well, it all comes in bits and pieces. I know we receive soul remembering as we are able to handle it in the moment. These experiences can be very intense."

Sarah continued, "So far, I remember what I did in my many life times in Lemuria. I know I was a Historian for several lives during these times and passionately collected and protected the ancient teachings of the Stars. I also worked with others on creating the DNA activation systems which are now being used to bring Lemuria back. The time is now. For a while I was working specifically with the Sirians and the Pleiadians. The planet Sirius is my home and I have a twin flame, Fiandra, who is Sirian. In a parallel life, she oversees the Crystalline Grid on Earth and works from a Sirian spaceship. Little do we know yet about what the Lemurian civilizations have left for us to discover underneath the Earth. Fiandra is also helping me to connect with the Lemurian Library to access the ancient wisdom of the Stars. The information I have received so far is about the power of Oneness; unity consciousness, love, compassion and that we are all Divine."

Sarah continued, "Recently, I found the place on Earth where Fiandra and I were last together before our soul split, during one of our Lemurian lifetimes. Yes, I found that place, which truly feels like home here on Earth now."

Sarah paused for a while, deep in thought and continued, "You know, this remembering process is very interesting. On one hand, you experience bliss because you finally find out who you truly are. On the other hand, you feel the pain, caused by separation from your star family, and you feel the desire of wanting to go home. Once you start realizing that it is all within, that there is only love and all is connected, you start co-creating 'Heaven on Earth'. I hope this answers your questions to some degree," Sarah concluded.

"Yes," Ronja replied, "Your stories resonated with me in many ways. Thank you for sharing. Do you think that speaking the Cosmic Language of Light to myself helps me with my DNA activation?" Ronja asked.

"Yes Ronja, speaking Light Language continuously to yourself and others helps with activations. The tools of Ascension include light, vibration and sound. You are on track, Ronja. Just be patient. All comes in at the right time," Sarah said and then left the room as she was guided to give them some time alone together.

Ronja was deep in thought when Ezrael asked her, "So what do you remember?"

Ronja was not sure if she should tell Ezrael about her recurrent dreams about him and decided not to share them at this moment. Instead, she told him about all the exciting new revelations and visions she had experienced so far.

He was very intrigued by all of Ronja's stories, although he could not fully grasp them all. If it weren't for hearing stories like these from his mom, he would probably think that she made everything up. Now, as he knew better, he understood where Ronja was coming from, and wished he could remember more too.

CHAPTER 7

The Recognition

Ronja found herself staring at Ezrael. She still could not believe that he was the boy she had seen over and over again in her dreams.

Ezrael felt uncomfortable under her gaze; not sure why though. He then became aware of Ronja's auric field and saw the similar structures and colors as he saw around his mom. He witnessed the golden and silver strands flowing from the heart to the pineal gland, vibrating and spinning, resembling DNA strands. She also emanated the deep emerald green color from her heart.

"Hmmm," Ezrael said, feeling more comfortable to share with Ronja, "since I woke up in the hospital yesterday, I see things which I have not seen before."

Ronja asked, "I would love to hear about what you are seeing, if you are willing to share."

Ezrael enjoyed being seen and heard and was actually quite excited to share his experiences with her. Being with Ronja was fun because of her happy, open nature. He was surprised by how much he shared so easily, as he saw himself as an introvert and usually kept his thoughts and feelings to himself. But with Ronja it was different. He described to her everything he could see and Ronja listened with excitement.

"Wow, this sounds exactly like what I see in my meditations. I cannot see it the way you do with open eyes, but I can see all of the same things with my third eye. I do not have control over when I see it, sometimes it just comes through," Ronja explained.

All of a sudden, a wave of energy came over Ezrael. He started to breathe deeply in and out of his mouth which he had learned helped him with this process.

Ronja looked at him and said, *"Mohanageta akado yedanaha mataka."*

As she said these words, Ezrael felt even more energy flowing in and felt the need to close his eyes. He saw a vision of himself and Ronja, with some other teenagers, riding on their dragons through the Cosmos.

He opened his eyes with surprise and said to her, "Oh my God, I am starting to remember! You are one of the ones I am working with in the Cosmos."

She looked at him with a smile and said, "Yes, that is correct. My cosmic name is SumuRa and you are Lazumar, one kind of a Master, I think. We have been working together for quite some time. Now we need to find the others, but then again, maybe they will find us?"

The boy thought to himself, "Could this be true that I am Master? I do not remember all of this yet."

As if Ronja was reading his mind, she said, "I am sure you will remember too, Ezrael. It may take some time, you know. DNA activations happen gradually, so we do not get too overwhelmed. Remember your Mom said something about this when she was talking to us earlier."

The energies continued to come into Ezrael and he wondered out loud, "What is happening to me? It feels like my feet and palms are on fire."

"Just continue to breath in and out through your mouth," Ronja explained and continued, "You are receiving downloads and what you are feeling is quite normal."

"Are these downloads always so intense?" Ezrael asked, "You barely seem to be affected by it, so I guess you must be used to it?"

"It is always different," Ronja explained, "I feel the energies coming in right now, although this time it does not feel as intense as it has in the past for me. I think these downloads are mainly for you."

"You know, I have seen you in many of my dreams," Ronja dared to share in that moment.

"What do you mean, I was in your dreams?" Ezrael asked with curiosity.

Ronja then shared everything with him. She told him about her many recurrent dreams where he was fighting the dark forces and came so close to winning. Ronja told him about how she saw Master Merlin and Novix in her dreams as well. Then, she described the last dream she had, and how he finally won by finding self-love and compassion.

Ezrael was deep in thought, "Hmm, the names, Master Merlin and Novix, sound familiar. That is all I recall right now."

"Don't force it, Ezrael," Ronja said. "The more we work together, the more it will come, and you will receive guidance about what to do next. We can also start meditating together and see if Master Merlin and Novix will come through again for you. Just do not be surprised if your Guides change as you go through this journey. This is quite possible as it happened to me."

"What do you mean?" Ezrael asked.

Ronja explained, "Well, I had Native American Spirit Guides, Elves and Devas at the beginning. After I woke up from the coma, my Spirit Guides changed to different Cosmic Light Beings and one from Inner Earth. Many believe the Guides are really our own energy configurations. Personally, I am not sure what to believe yet."

"This all sounds very exciting," Ezrael said with a hint of frustration. "When are my Guides going to show up to let me know what I am supposed to be doing next?" he wondered out loud.

"No worries, you are always doing your multidimensional work whether you are aware of it or not. The remembering will come when it comes, at the perfect time. Right now, you need to recover and integrate these new energies. Just relax and take it day by day," Ronja said.

"I feel you are right, thank you. Maybe we can hang out sometimes?" Ezrael asked shyly. "I am feeling like I really need support at the moment from people like you who understand me and what I am going through."

"Sure, I would love to and it's all part of the grand plan. I am looking forward to meeting the others as well. We will all be working together as a team soon. In fact, let's get started. Are you up to doing a meditation together now?" Ronja asked.

"Absolutely!" Ezrael said with excitement.

Ronja started, "Let us close our eyes for a moment and take a few deep breaths together. Let us have the intention to connect with our Spirit Guides to gain some insights on what we are to do going forward."

"Merlin, he is ready," Novix stated. "How fast he is willing to connect with us again. I am so excited."

"Yes!" Merlin said with joyous laughter. "He is our boy alright! So Merlin, closed his eyes, took his wand and created a whirlwind of golden and silver sparkles.

Ezrael and Ronja felt a lot of energies coming in and Ezrael said, "Oh my God, I see all this golden-silver color coming into our bodies. They look like sparkles. Oh my God, it is so beautiful to see! Now these energies are surrounding our bodies and making their way into our hearts."

Ronja could not see any of this; although she felt the energies in her body, which was a confirmation for her of what he was describing. She also felt the heat in her palms and feet.

Suddenly, she received a knowing and said, "We need to find the others! It is time. I am guided to walk through the town today and I feel like I am going to find another one of us. I am supposed to go right now."

Merlin and Novix smiled at each other and Novix said, "Yep, she got the message! They received the downloads! It is fun to see how fast Humans respond to our energies when they work together! It is fascinating!"

She immediately opened her eyes and suggested they exchange phone numbers, which they did. They agreed to meet again tomorrow afternoon for another meditation. When they said goodbye, Ronja promised to text Ezrael if she found the other person in town.

Ronja said goodbye to Sarah as well and gave her a big long hug.

Sarah said, "Please keep me in the loop about what is going on. I know you have your own work to do together and I would like to be part of the process."

Ronja felt good about it, especially because she thought having some guidance from Sarah would be very helpful and all of them working together seemed more powerful anyway.

When Sarah opened the door for Ronja to leave, Sarah quickly held Ronja's hand, looked into her eyes and said, "Gonamaheta!"

In the same moment, Ronja felt a blast of energy in her heart and she understood the translation of Sarah's Light Language to be, "The Crystal Store."

Ronja could not believe what just happened. She thanked Sarah, embraced her one more time and off Ronja went into town to visit the only metaphysical store which carried crystals. The store's name was "The Seeing".

As Ronja walked towards the town, she felt so excited. She knew she was actually starting out on an adventure which she had always dreamed about.

CHAPTER 8

The Uniting

It did not take Ronja long to walk to the metaphysical store, "The Seeing". As she entered the shop, she felt the intense energies emitted from hundreds of crystals. An older man, with white hair and a beard, was sitting behind a counter and welcomed her.

Ronja was disappointed because she was hoping to find someone her age, who would be part of their new team. However, she decided to trust the Universe, stay present and be open.

"How can I help you?" the old man asked in a friendly voice.

"Well Sir, I am not sure if you can help me," Ronja stated, "I was guided to come here to meet someone who works with crystals and the only one here is you. No disrespect, Sir, I am looking for someone younger, close to my age."

The man started laughing and said, "It seems like I am not good enough for your mission." He continued to laugh and said, "I love this new generation of young people. You just know what you want and need. I am not offended though, love, and I might know the person you are looking for."

He looked to the back of the store and shouted, "Kai! Kai! Please come out front. Someone is looking for you!"

Ronja was surprised and excited to see a boy with brown hair and brown eyes come forward. He seemed to be very close to her age.

"Yes, Grandpa, what can I help you with?" the boy asked.

"This young lady is looking for you," the old man said.

As the boy approached her with curiosity, Ronja was not sure how to respond. She just held out her hand to greet him and said, "Yes, my name is Ronja and I guess your name is Kai."

He shook her hand and responded in a surprisingly deep voice, "Yes, that is me." All of a sudden Ronja felt a surge of energy flowing through her body and she needed to breath deeper to help these energies to integrate.

She took one step back and looked at him. She had a vision of him carrying a sword of light and flying through the Cosmos on a large, blue dragon. She saw him surrounded by many other dragons, all flying together.

"Are you ok?" he asked.

"Yes, I think so," she said not really knowing what more to say in that moment.

The boy was curious and asked, "Why are you here?"

"I was guided to come here to find you. You are one of Us," Ronja said.

Now he was really intrigued and asked, "Who is Us?'

"Well…," Ronja paused for a moment, "We are not really sure about it all, ourselves. The only thing I do know is that it is time to find each other because we have some work to do for the planet. I feel we will know more and get clear instructions when we all gather together," Ronja replied.

The old man, who was witnessing this conversation, disappeared behind the counter to give the children privacy to converse.

Ronja continued, "I received an insight that I would meet someone here today, who works with crystals and creates crystal grids."

"That is exactly what I have been doing for the past two years," Kai responded with excitement. "Crystals just keep coming to me and I have been creating crystal grids like crazy. I am creating them wherever and whenever I am guided to," he said.

"I would like to get to know you and your group better because it feels really right," Kai continued.

Ronja had to smile. She felt a very good connection with this boy and said, "Do you have time to meet tomorrow?"

Kai replied, "Yes, of course. I will make the time. Just tell me when and where."

"Okay, great!" Ronja said excitedly. "So far, it is only four of us. Let me text Ezrael, to see if he has time to meet tomorrow."

Ezrael response immediately was a "yes". They all agreed to meet at 3 pm at Ezrael's house. Ronja gave him the address and they exchanged phone numbers. She invited Kai to bring his crystals if he felt inspired.

Before Ronja left, she just could not help herself and asked, "Are you familiar with dragons?"

Kai's mouth dropped open and he said after a pause, "Wow." His expression was a combination of disbelief and awe. Then he replied, "Yep, we are definitely meant to work together."

In the next moment, a customer entered the store and Kai said, "We will have so much to talk about tomorrow! I am looking forward to it."

Ronja said goodbye and left the store. On her way home, she felt so excited. She had just received such an amazing confirmation that she could trust and rely on her Visions and her "Inner Knowing".

Suddenly, she noticed the hundreds of butterflies flying in the fields around her and became aware of the wind gently caressing her face. She knew the butterflies were a message from her parents and she felt their presence in her heart. A wave of emotion came over her and she started to cry with intense grief over the loss of her parents. She learned over the past year, that grieving was something that came intensely at times and then would leave as unexpectedly as it appeared, similar to an ocean wave.

Ronja thanked her parents for this beautiful message and deep in her heart she knew that they were supporting her from the other side. This was another confirmation that she was on track and that the work with the team was going to be significant.

CHAPTER 9

The Pleiadian Transmission

Ezrael's father, Peter, arrived shortly after Ronja left for the crystal store. Peter asked to talk with Sarah alone, and they sat down in the living room. Peter looked at Sarah and said with a stern voice, "Although I could never understand all the spiritual work you do, I always supported and encouraged you."

Sarah listened, fully present, as he continued, "This time it involves our son. We almost lost him. I am here to ask you to stop all of this spiritual stuff for Ezrael's sake. I would like to take him to stay with me for the rest of the summer. Carina can take off from work and he will be in good hands with us."

Peter continued, "I feel like he needs a break from all this energy stuff so he can just have a normal life and get better. What do you think?"

Sarah, knowing this was coming, calmly replied, "Well, I do understand where you are coming from, Peter. But our son's spiritual journey has just begun and I am not sure if there is anything we can do to stop it, even if we try."

Peter wondered out loud, "Are you saying he will turn out just like you? Doing ceremonies, facilitating groups and doing healing work? I do not wish that for our son. It is important that he keeps his focus on his education and does not get distracted from his real life path."

Sarah replied, "Our son has always been a good student and I am not worried about him finishing high school, and of course he will go to college, Peter. His spiritual path has nothing to do with that, both paths can coexist together. As parents, our role is to support him in making his own decisions. We want him to follow the path that brings him the most joy and fulfillment. Have you asked him what he would like to do over the summer?"

Sarah continued, "The plan was that we will switch in two weeks, right after the solar eclipse. I would like to continue with our original agreement unless Ezrael decides he would like to stay with you starting now. If this is the case, of course I have nothing against it."

"Whether you want to see it or not, Spirit has reached out to Ezrael and he has started on his spiritual path already," Sarah explained, "I am well equipped to guide him through this awakening process if he asks me for my assistance."

Peter agreed, "You are right. Let us talk to him now and see what he would like to do. If he wants to stay at your house, then I will continue to check in on him on a more regular basis."

"Thank you for understanding, Peter," Sarah said.

"Alright then, let us talk to him," Peter said, feeling a little bit better now that they were both sort of on the same page.

As they entered the room, Ezrael was resting. He opened his eyes and smiled as soon as he saw his father and said, "Dad! How good to see you."

They hugged and Peter asked, "How are you feeling?"

"I feel still a little tired, otherwise better than ever before." Ezrael smiled and continued, "I honestly feel like I was reborn. I feel so much lighter and happier, and I am not really sure why. I feel totally whole and more accepting of who I am."

Peter replied, "Ezrael, I am very glad to hear this. However, we are a little concerned about you after what just happened. Carina and I thought it would be a good idea for you to stay with us for the next few weeks. Carina can take off work to be with you during the day. We can make it a restful time before we go on our vacation together. Your mom is okay with this plan if it sounds good to you. What do you think?"

Ezrael knew where his father was coming from. Ezrael thought back about how he also resisted all the spiritual stuff his mom was involved in and how he never wanted to learn anything she wanted to share with him. For the first time he was curious about the spiritual world and was open to learn more.

Therefore, he replied, "Thank you for the offer, Dad, but I would like to stay with Mom for the next two weeks as we have agreed on. I am getting a lot of rest here and right now I am opening up to something that is bigger than me. I know Mom can help and guide me through this process. It is something that I do not want to stop. For the first time in my life, I feel alive, Dad. I would like to continue connecting to like-minded people. I truly feel like there is more to life than I have been able to perceive, and I am excited to explore this further."

"Alright, Ezrael," Peter said in acceptance. "This is your choice. I would like to see you as often as I can, otherwise I will call you every day to check in on how you are doing."

"Okay, sounds good," Ezrael replied, understanding where he was coming from. Ezrael felt that he had the best Dad ever and was grateful being so loved by his parents and Dad's new wife.

Sarah asked Peter, "Would you and Carina like to come for dinner tomorrow or the next day?"

"I will talk to Carina and get back to you. Thank you, that is a very good idea," Peter replied.

"Perfect," Sarah stated.

After saying their goodbyes, Peter left.

Sarah returned to Ezrael and asked him if he needed anything. Ezrael looked at his mom and said, "I am sorry that I always gave you such a hard time about your divorce and blamed you for everything that happened."

Sarah replied, "Oh, Ezrael, you don't have to apologize. You were upset and you needed to take it out on someone. I do understand." Sarah gave her son a big hug and continued, "We all love you so much. I hope you know that, Ezrael. We all grew up believing that there is only one family structure that is healthy. Children often tend to believe that it is their fault and I hope you know it never had anything to do with you. It is more important that we follow our inner guidance and heart to stay in alignment, even though it can hurt some of us in the process of changing to a situation that will ultimately be for the highest good of all. Look at how happy your father is now with Carina and how happy I am now that I found my soul tribe."

"What do you mean by staying in alignment, Mom?" Ezrael asked.

Sarah responded, "When we are fully present in the moment, with an open heart and mind, the spirit messages come through as an 'Inner Knowing', which shows me exactly the next step ahead. Well, at least that is how it works for me. Sometimes our mind wants to know what lies ahead and the future steps, when the true gift is being present in the 'NOW'. We are opening up to a Quantum Consciousness, where everything we need to know in the moment can be accessed in the 'Now'. This is where we align with all different dimensions, our multidimensional Higher Selves and start creating 'Heaven on Earth' with our childlike innocence and imagination. That is the magic we all possess. Even Einstein talks about this."

Ezrael was intrigued and asked, "What do you mean by different dimensions and multidimensional Higher Selves?"

Sarah answered, "Our soul has many different dimensional aspects. We were programed to believe we only live in this 3D reality and were never allowed to even consider the possibility of our existence on other dimensional realities. For example, we may also have a parallel existence living on a spaceship or even on another planet. When we start going within and exploring the space within us, we start awakening to the different aspects of ourselves, of our soul. Since time is an illusion, we can have many realities occurring simultaneously on the different dimensional planes. The more we disconnect from the Matrix and the mind control programing, the more we evolve and become aware of these mysteries of the Universe.

All souls are part of the highest dimension, God-Source, and we can access this high energy aspect of ourselves through our Higher Self, the all-knowing part of us that knows all of our lives, our gifts and helps us to remember who we truly are as multidimensional beings. I believe that most of us are Starseeds and the ones, who are awake and aware at this time, are not originally from this planet...But this is for another time."

Suddenly a rush of energies flowed through Sarah and she started to breath heavily in and out through her mouth and then spoke in Light Language, *"Adaheda Aka, Godonahe madeta gonadeta aka,"* and then she translated, "The Pleiadians are here for you, to give you a transmission to help you remember. Would you like to receive it, Ezrael?" Sarah asked.

Ezrael felt the high energies already coming in through his crown and agreed with excitement. He closed his eyes, while his mom continued to channel the Cosmic Language of Light and toning, *"Akaheda Nomada Godaheda! Madageta Adaheata Anaka! Gostareda! Aaaahhhhmmmmmmmmmmmmmmmmm!*

Mmmmmmhhhhhhhhhhhhhhhhhhhhhhhhhhhhhhhhhhhhhhhhhhhhhhhhhhhhhhh!"

Ezrael saw his third eye opening and felt heat and the flow of energy increasing in his crown chakra. At the same time, he saw and felt energies coming in the back of his head, flowing into the inside of his head and then out through his crown. Suddenly, he saw a tall, beautiful woman appear. She had long, blond hair and bright blue eyes.

The woman smiled at him and started to speak, "Lazumar (Ezrael), my name is Dhalia. I am a Pleiadian Priestess and I am here to give you the gift of your Pleiadian DNA activation. We have already agreed in another dimension to work together, and it has started."

Dhalia continued, "You are from the Stars, Lazumar. You are a Lemurian Master. The Cosmos is home to you and you know it well, as do all the members of your Star Team here on Earth. You are Pleiadian and we had many life times in Lemuria together. We, the Lemurian Council of the Cosmic Heart & Light, have trained you in the mystic laws of the Stars until you actually have taught us. Yes, we are here to activate your soul remembrance to help us bring the true energies of Lemuria back to this planet now. The energies of NEW EARTH are of the 5th Dimensional frequency, 5D, as humans understand and refer to it in their linear thinking. These energies are based on Love, Compassion and Unity Consciousness. It is time to help humans disconnect from the Matrix of fear. It is time to move people away from suffering and out of the illusion of separation. We are but ONE, all coming from God Source. We are here to support humankind at this critical time of the Ascension."

Dhalia instructed, "You will bring this activation to your Star Team first. They are all Lemurians as well. You will relay this transmission to your Star Team exactly as I instruct you to do now: Put the tip of your tongue on the roof of your mouth, close your bottom muscles and create a *'MMMMhhh'* sound. You will feel the vibration of this sound on your lips which will confirm the frequency is flowing properly. You will know when the activation is complete."

Dhalia continued, "We deeply honor and love you, Lazumar, and we are excited to work with you again."

In the next moment, Dhalia bowed and left his awareness.

Exactly as Dhalia disappeared, Sarah stopped toning and speaking the Cosmic Language of Light. She opened her eyes, smiled at Ezrael and said, "Wow, this was a very big transmission!"

"Yes, Mom," Ezrael smiled back at her and continued, "I just received a DNA transmission from the Pleiadians. I also gained fascinating insights about who I am on another dimension. The Pleiadians help me remember and want to guide and work with me!"

After Ezrael briefly shared their experiences with his mom, Sarah brought him a large glass of water and some soup. She suggested that he rest for a while. Sarah reminded him to drink a lot of water over the next few days to help integrate the energies into his physical body. It was not long before Ezrael fell sound asleep, looking forward to tomorrow's afternoon meeting with his new friends.

Little did Ezrael know that his Mom also received instructions and a powerful activation from Dhalia as well. His Mom had been working with Dhalia and the Sirians for quite some time. It was now time for her to step up on her mission as well. It was her work to open the two time capsules during the Solar Eclipse; this was to be the game changer.

CHAPTER 10

The Infiltration

Imero and Ammagant were settled back in Imero's study. Neither one felt completely content with the results of the Inner Earth meeting.

Imero was worried about the Lemurians and said, "I am concerned about the Gedoha Clan's strategy. Just having one strategy to shift the energies during the dark phase of the solar eclipse does not guarantee we will be successful in taking back our power. Let us not forget that the Matrix is not fully functioning at this time. We need another plan to assure we will succeed."

In the next moment, they both felt a cold wind and Ammagant said, "I think we are getting a visitor."

Suddenly, a dark figure appeared. He was about 7 feet tall, slim and wore a black cloak with a hood that covered his head and hid his face. His energy felt very cold and creepy, even to Ammagant and Imero. Although they never met this being before, they knew exactly who he was. His name was Occuna, the Dark Emperor of the Galaxies.

Imero greeted him in a friendly way, although he wanted to make sure he was recognized as the powerful dark leader on Planet Earth, "Occuna, what a surprise. Welcome to my Kingdom. What brings you here?"

Occuna started to talk in a stern and metallic voice, "I am keenly aware of what is going on here on Earth. This is very disturbing to me. What happens on Planet Earth affects all in our Galaxy. I am here to give you my advanced technology to help you assure the interference of lower vibrations is transmitted at the highest capacity."

Imero became very excited and replied, "What kind of technology?"

The dark figure manifested instruments that looked like a tablet and a cell phone, along with another device that looked like a pen.

"What are these things?" Imero asked with curiosity.

Occuna explained, "These are infiltration systems. They work very fast and are quite effective."

"Tell us more!" Imero exclaimed.

The Dark Emperor of the Galaxy continued, "These devices connect to all cell phones, computers and tablets on your planet. Once this system is programmed, all personal electronic devices will transmit lower vibrational energies to receptive humans and Starseeds. This will be especially effective for lowering the frequencies and abilities of the Starseed Children, who are more sensitive and receptive to these energies. It will prevent these children from remembering their multidimensional Higher Selves, and what their powers are. It will freeze their imagination. I am confident it will block their connection to Gaia and to the God-Source energies. Of course, it does the same for the adults, as well as amplify fear."

"Can you explain a little bit more?" Imero asked.

Occuna replied, "Of course! I love nothing more than to talk about my inventions." He laughed and continued, "These frequencies create addictions to these devices and more importantly, calcifications in the viewer's pineal gland. As you know, Imero, this small gland in the middle of the brain is the doorway to connecting to the different dimensions. Transmitting through these personal devices works better than any kind of implant because it is untraceable. In only three minutes, this transmission will significantly impact the pineal gland. In a week or two, the majority of people on the planet will be completely disconnected from the energy grids of Earth, imagination will be stopped, and the divine spark of each person will be negligible. Then they will be completely controlled through your Matrix Mind Control System again."

"This sounds very intriguing," Imero said, "You are known for your mastery in advanced technologies and I trust you will deliver. I would like to employ this system as soon as possible, especially if we can re-establish mind control."

Imero had one more question, "So who would not be affected by the transmissions from this technology?"

Occuna paused for a second. He wanted to be careful in his reply, so as not to lose the deal, "Well, as you know, there are some highly advanced Starseeds. Their DNA works on a higher frequency and many are already out of mind control. They are not subject to addiction to their tablets and cell phones and their pineal glands are already highly activated. Many are the Lemurians, who have agreed to incarnate in this crucial time to help with the Ascension, cannot be affected by it. I am aware that they have started to unite. There is nothing we can do about these Lemurians at this time. They are also protected and supported by teams in many dimensions and Galaxies. Because these Lemurians are Masters of the Quantum Field, not many are needed to make a huge impact in raising the frequencies of all on Earth and in the Galaxy. Our only hope is to drastically lessen the remembering process of those Starseeds who are still asleep. At the same time it is important to drastically reduce the frequency of the humans with fear, so there will be no way for the light to overpower the dark. We have a short window of time, so I would suggest starting as soon as possible, as more and more Starseeds are being activated daily."

Imero, now frowning, replied, "This is very concerning. So this technology is not a fool proof solution after all. However, I do not think we have a choice at this time. We must do everything in our power to make sure we succeed!"

"When can we start?" Imero asked.

"We can start it now, if you wish," Occuna replied.

"Yes, let us start immediately. We do not have any time to waste!" Imero agreed.

Occuna gave Imero the devices and instructed, "You, Imero, will have to do this for me. Wait until you are sure I am off the planet before you press the green button on each instrument once. As soon as you press the green button one time, it will start blinking orange for three minutes until the infiltration is done. Do not touch anything during the transmission period! When the orange blinking light turns to green, the transmission has been completed. Immediately after all buttons turn green, destroy all three devices. It is very important that this infiltration will not be traced back to me. Is that clear?"

Imero replied, "Yes, it is crystal clear, Occuna. It is best for you to leave now, so I can fulfill this mission! Thank you, Occuna, for your brilliant technology."

Occuna replied, "I will visit again and observe from afar! The trade for this will be negotiated the next time I see you. Do not make any mistakes!"

Occuna disappeared in a split second.

Imero and Ammagant were waiting patiently to give Occuna enough time to leave the space of Earth. They were excited to start the infiltration.

CHAPTER 11

The First Gathering

Ronja was excited about the meeting with Sarah, Ezrael and Kai this afternoon. She could not explain why, but she felt uneasy today. She felt an urgency that something needed to be done.

Just before she left her friend Nina called. Ronja got the hit to invite her to the meeting. Nina was not really sure if that would be something for her, as she was not like Ronja, who was very open to the unseen world. Something sounded intriguing and therefore Nina answered, "Yes."

Nina lived close by. They arranged to meet in the afternoon. For Ronja every minute passed too slowly. But finally, it was time. Ronja picked up her friend, and off they went to Sarah's house to meet the others.

Sarah opened the door and welcomed Ronja and Nina into the house. Ezrael was already excited to be meeting Ronja again. He was surprised to see Nina and welcomed her. Ronja shared with them how she met Kai yesterday and all were excited to meet him as well. As soon as she told them about Kai, the doorbell rang and Kai was joining. Kai brought his favorite crystals in his backpack just in case they were needed today. It was very heavy. Sarah brought in a candle, lit it and burned some incense. She invited all of them to sit in a circle together on the floor and to hold hands.

Next, Sarah said, "Welcome to our first meeting. I am welcoming you all in the circle. We all are unique, divine expressions, multidimensional, heart open and gifted. Nothing is a coincidence. We were called together to be of service for Planet Earth and the Cosmos. We do not need to understand what we have to do because our brain won't be able to comprehend it anyways. Are you willing to try something new?" Sarah asked.

All of them were curious, open and they agreed.

Sarah continued, "So, let us use toning to create a specific energy. Toning is the unique essence of your soul which comes through as a sound you create. Each of you will create a different tone; meaning your own unique sound. Let us start by dropping into our hearts and through our toning we will unite our energies and invoke higher, benevolent frequencies."

Sarah started by toning an *"Aaaaaaaaaaaaaaaaaaahhh"* sound and all the others joined in with their own unique tones. As they continued on for a while, the combined sound of them started to shift and it resonated with each other.

They felt energies flowing through their bodies and heat in their hands and feet. Next, increased energy was entering from the back of their neck, flowing into their pineal gland and then up and out through the crown chakra.

After a while it became silent and Sarah started to speak in the Cosmic Language of Light, *"Godeheda Madaka Deda Minu Avatar. Getaha maka. Ostamaheda nogada."*

As Sarah spoke, they felt an energy increase in the field and a heart opening. Ronja had tears in her eyes. She felt this "love energy" and the familiar feeling of "home" again.

Kai suddenly spoke in Light Language for the first time, *"Mimmmi mmimiimimi miiimmiiimii miimimimmmmmmmm."*

Ronja started speaking as well, *"Ochtaka Echtonoda Machadoeka."*

Nina was not sure what this was all about. However, it felt very familiar to her. Suddenly, she had a vision and started to share, "Oh goodness gracious! I see all of us riding through the Cosmos on dragons. This is all very new to me, but I thought I would share."

Sarah said, "Please continue, Nina. What do you see?"

Nina continued, "We are traveling to a specific place. I am not sure where or what it is called. But it is beautiful. It looks magical. Oh my God! There are many crystalline high towers and pyramids. I do not understand why, but I now have the "Inner Knowing" that this place is called Lemuria. Now we are landing and many different Cosmic Light Beings are presenting themselves and forming a circle around us. A tall, beautiful Light Being is stepping forward and speaking, *"Medaga Aheta Godona. Enaahate Madadeka aka. Estadoda nemanoda Ezrael eda Lazumar."*

All of a sudden, Nina was able to translate the words into English. She was surprised at her new ability and continued, "We need to help Ezrael remember. He is Lazumar!"

Ezrael said, "I do not understand. Who is Lazumar?"

Nina continued to relay the light language messages from the beautiful Light Being and translated, *"Godaheda manakada gedoha!* He is our Lemurian Master and when he finds out who he is, he will shift the energy on this planet with the help of all of you."

Ronja was excited to hear this and said, *"Machtuda Nokachemako dachadecha ochtana."*

Kai replied with, *"Miimii mimiiimiiim mimmimiimimmmimiiiiiiiiiiiii!* We are all ONE and the gift of 'remembering who we are' is within us."

Ezrael felt frustrated, as he was the only one in the group who did not speak this Language of Light yet. After a short pause he asked, "Why me? Why can I not remember?"

Nina responded with the answer from the Cosmic Light Being, *"Manaheta godanota ektaka. Dodaneha mahagoda aka! Madahoda enamagata Ejahada nodamaneahata Ga!* There is a reason for this, Ezrael. The dark forces are doing everything possible to keep you from remembering. Do not fear! We are here to help you. You will remember what you need to know in the very moment. The information will always come exactly on time. Trust in divine timing and just be patient. *Godanamaka edoha anama dodeha godenata aka.* Do not underestimate your powers. All of you are starting to work in the Quantum Field, and this is the Game Changer. All will be revealed in the perfect time. Just trust and believe."

Nina continued, "*Godanota ehadota aka. Elohim maneta odahema Dodona manaheta godinata edanaha godena. Enahagata madagoda adanaheta maga!* You are the Starseeds! You are the Lemurians, who are bringing in the wisdom for a new world. Start meditating daily together and call us in. We are the Lemurian Council of the Cosmic Heart and Light. Our members include representatives from the Sirian, Arcturian and Pleiadian Star Systems. We have worked with you for eons, as we have had many missions together."

Nina continued to speak and translate, "*Edoctaheda nonamada godoahoda nataheda aka. Menokada gedahadeda dodaheada manahata godehna. Aktaheda Manogada Ehhhhakada Godaheda Nonadedagadaha.* It is urgent at the moment. The dark forces will increase the low vibrational energies on Earth. Now, we ask you to use your imagination and intend to send 'high frequency love vibration' out through all electronic communication devices! There is no time to waste! We will explain more at another time. *Magadoaheda gatanada menobada akaheda goradehada nodaka.* Create a crystal grid and send love and light through all electronic devices now!"

Kai instantly got out all his crystals from his backpack and created a crystal grid right in the center of their circle. All of a sudden, he had a vision that he was holding a light sword in his hand. His sapphire blue dragon flew to his side and soon he was surrounded by many other dragons. Kai started speaking in a loud voice, which represented the dragons, "*Sotaitehe! Naheischtehe! Gemaheischtede!*" While Kai was speaking, he moved his hand over the crystal grid.

They all intuitively knew that this was the time to envision sending love and light. They saw and felt the energies flowing through their hearts into this grid and then out to all the electronic devices. The all felt the energies intensify in the circle.

After a long moment of silence, Nina continued to tell them about what was happening in her vision, "The Cosmic Light Beings are thanking us and leaving now. We are taking off with our dragons and returning home."

Although all seemed done, Ezrael remembered the instructions from yesterday to share the Pleiadian transmission with his friends. He did not hesitate and said, "I have received a Pleiadian Transmission and I was instructed to share it with you. Put the tip of your tongue on the roof of your mouth, close your bottom muscles and create a *'MMMMhhh'* sound. You will feel the vibration of this sound on your lips which will confirm the frequency is flowing properly. You will know when the activation is complete."

All were excited to follow his instructions and were humming for a while until the download felt complete.

They stayed in sacred silence for another few minutes, integrating the energies and giving their minds time to process all that had just transpired. It felt like the start of an adventure they had all been waiting to begin.

Sarah suggested to close the circle with toning again, which they did. This time their sounds felt even stronger and more united. After toning, they gave thanks and felt a profound sense of awe. It was a while before anyone spoke, as the energies surrounding them were so beautiful and no one wanted to leave this blissful state.

Finally, Ronja said, "Wow, Nina! This was amazing. I had no idea you had such gifts. I am so glad you joined us today!"

Nina's eyes welled with tears and she said, "Thank you, Ronja. I never knew that I was capable of doing anything like that. Today something magical happened. For the first time, I felt my powers and connected to something that felt so familiar, like I had done this many times before. I know now that I am a Seer. I always had the feeling that something was missing in my life and I know I found it today. I heard the Cosmic Light Beings calling me Lalunar, and it felt right."

Kai spoke with heartfelt enthusiasm, "This is wonderful to hear, Nina! Thank you for sharing your new-found gift with us! Nothing is a coincidence. You were definitely meant to be here today with us!"

Kai continued, "I was quite excited to hear myself speaking Light Language for the first time! Plus, I was so happy to have my crystals ready to create the grid. It made carrying that heavy backpack all the way here totally worth it. I know I am to continue working with the crystal grids during our gatherings. We are all here to support each other! Everything is possible when we work together. Without you guys I might have not spoken Light Language for the first time. This is all very exciting! Thank you!"

"One for All and All for One!" Ezrael replied, and they all laughed. "You are quite gifted, Kai. You must be our Wizard and Dragon Master," Ezrael said.

"Yes, I think you may be right," Kai replied with a huge smile on his face. "This all started two years ago, when my grandfather asked me to help out in his crystal store after school. I became intensely connected to the crystals, they sort of talked to me. Then I started having dreams about a blue dragon continuously. I felt the need to connect with this dragon in meditation and finally, one day, it happened. My dragon, Goran, came in and started sharing his wisdom with me. After we got to know each other, Goran started introducing me to many other dragons and I now work with them all. It has only been a couple months since I started creating grids. It felt like I was struck by lightning yesterday, when Ronja asked if I work with grids and dragons! Of course, it was a no brainer that I had to meet all of you. I feel so blessed to be working with you on this mission."

Kai paused for a moment, and then asked, "Ezrael, how was the meditation for you?"

Ezrael replied, "Very interesting! This is all new to me too. I also have a gift of sight but mine is different from Nina's. Since I woke up in the hospital, a few days ago, I see energies with open eyes, in the form of colors, grid patterns and symbols. Today, during the meditation, I saw golden energies emanating from the crystal grid, which Kai created. I also saw huge beams of white light flowing down and around each of us in the group. I was mesmerized by this beautiful sight."

Ezrael paused, as he experienced these beams again, and then continued, "I saw small geometric symbols floating around us within these beams of light. In particular, I noticed golden Ankhs and Infinity symbols spinning at a very fast speed as they floated around us in our light columns. They seemed to emanate golden sparkles in all directions as they spun. Also, it just hit me, that I saw an emerald green color in all of our hearts. This emerald green is different from the grass green color which I have been seeing in most other people's hearts."

"Wow, Ezrael," Sarah said with excitement. "This is amazing. I did not know that this gift came to you since your hospital encounter. I was wondering what gifts you have received since then. This is exciting news. I feel your new sight will help you and this group in every moment."

Sarah suggested they set up a time to start meditating together on a daily basis as they were guided by the Light Being. They agreed to meet by phone at 6 am each morning. Sarah immediately set up the conference call number and texted them the details. They knew they would be meeting in person often and the times would be revealed.

Sarah offered them a snack, then went outside into her medicine wheel structure and sat down. She was guided to light a candle outside and offer some tobacco for honoring the Ancestors and Mother Gaia. Sarah had received new messages during this meeting instructing her on how to work with the two time capsules. She was not surprised to hear about the interference being implemented by the dark forces. Instead of feeling worried about it, she trusted and believed that love and light will always be stronger than the dark. She trusted that all the support of the Light Beings of the Galaxies will help them in their task ahead.

CHAPTER 12

Powering up of all Forces

Imero finally received the knowing that Occuna was clearly out of the Planet Earth Space. Imero grinned at Ammagant and said, "I think it is time! It is time to get everything back into our hands!"

Ammagant and Imero sat down together and, thanks to Occuna's instructions, Imero knew exactly what he had to do. He opened the glass lids on the three devices, which all displayed a green light, just as Occuna had explained.

Then Imero, with a huge smile on his face, pressed all three green buttons. As soon as he did, the three green lights turned orange and started blinking. Suddenly, everything started to shake and energies, which they had never experienced before, were being powerfully transmitted from these devices to the Earth. These energies connected to all TVs, computers and cell phones instantly. He remembered that this transmission would take three Earth minutes to be completed.

Imukah, the Mechanical Engineer and controller of the codes and transmissions from the Central Sun, was a little surprised when all of a sudden an alarm went off. He looked at the central control screen and said, "Here we go again. Another trial of interference of the dark forces has started. I must remember to thank them for keeping my job a little more exciting."

He quickly went to work to counteract these energies by increasing other transmissions, but it did not seem to work yet. Imukah telepathically connected to the Lemurian Council Members of the Cosmic Heart & Light to send them an update. This kind of challenge did not affect Imukah at all, as he was the Master Creator of all transmissions and codes of the Omniverse. He was well known for his brilliant, logical mind and clear focus in handling all that happens in the Omniverse, no matter what circumstances arise. Keeping everything in perfect synchronistic order was his mission and passion; he loved every minute of it.

It was almost 6 am the next morning and Sarah had started preparing for the conference call. Suddenly something felt different, and she had the knowing that this call was needed to counteract dark forces. Sarah created a sacred space again with incense and candles, not knowing that Kai was doing the same in his home. Kai was guided to work with crystals and created a beautiful crystal grid with an Ankh symbol in the middle. As he completed his grid he started speaking Light Language into it, *"Miiiimiiimiiiih mimiimiiihhhh mimimmiiiiihmmi mimmiimimiiiiiii."*

Sarah sat down in her healing room, closed her eyes and opened the Akashic Records to seal the space and to receive guidance from the Akash. The Akashic Records was an energy of consciousness, which Sarah had been working with for quite some time. Accessing these energies had helped Sarah and her clients to heal soul woundings and to receive information, which supported the awakening process. Opening these records always helped her to have a better connection with Spirit.

By surprise, Buddha Ganesh came to her in a vision and said, "My name is Buddha Ganesh, Anukha, which was Sarah's galactic name. I am here to keep your phone lines clear. I will help you transmute the negative energies, amplify all benevolent energies and support the peace movement here on Earth. I am the mayor of Inner Earth. Please speak now in the Cosmic Language of Light and we will clear the phone lines together!"

Sarah followed his instructions and spoke in a loud strong voice, *"Godaneha aka. Metanaha godaeha astadoda genamahata okanama!"*

When she stopped speaking, she got the information from Buddha Ganesh that the phone lines had been cleared.

In the next moment, Ezrael joined his mom in the healing room. It was time to call into the conference line. Kai, Nina and Ronja were already on the line waiting.

Sarah opened the meditation immediately, "Welcome everyone. Let us close our eyes and take few deep breaths with deepest gratitude for our body. Let us send a grounding cord from your navel down to the Crystalline Grid of the Earth, and it is being received with unconditional love from Mother Gaia. We are grounded to Earth. We are grounded to Earth. We are grounded to Earth. Now, let us connect our hearts together with the Cosmic Heart. We are calling in the North, the East, the South and the West; Father Sun, Grandfather Sky, Grandmother Moon, the animals, our Higher Selves, all our Guides and Guardians who work with us, all Ascended Masters, the highest, benevolent frequencies of the Pleiadians, Sirians, Arcturians and the Lemurian Council of the Cosmic Heart & Light. I am guided to create a very specific portal, which we will call "ESS". It will connect the Earth (E), Central Sun (S) and Sirius (S) through the Lion's Gate Portal, which is the gateway between them.

Sarah paused for a moment and then continued, "Oh yes, and Buddha Ganesh would like to join us. He wants to help us to purify, transmute, and amplify our energies as we intend to send peace to all on the Earth. Thank you for joining, Buddha Ganesh, Mayor of the Inner Earth! Now, let us tone together in unity and harmony. With our toning, let us open the ESS portal with the activation code number 1!"

Everyone knew what to do and they started toning together. The toning went on for quite some time. It became louder and louder. They soon felt a connection to the many other benevolent Cosmic Light Beings, who came in to work with them.

Imero and Ammagant enjoyed the powerful, dark energies coming in from the Interference. After a while, the orange blinking lights stopped and turned back to green. The transmission was complete! They had received telepathic report that the battery charging station was back up to 90%.

Imero started laughing and said, "That was easy! I love when the most powerful things are the easiest ones to establish. We do not have to work hard to get big things done. Now I have my power back on Planet Earth. I feel stronger than ever before and no one will escape my dark force," he screamed into the air.

Imukah diligently worked on his computer, constantly checking his screens as he put in different codes and number sequences, yet, nothing was working to stop the alarm. He was quantumly connecting to all beings, who were able to give him the fastest information to make snap, confident decisions about what to do.

Imukah suddenly had the amazing idea to create a bridge that looked like a rainbow. He saw each end of the Rainbow Bridge grounded in very specific places at the two poles of the Earth. The codes to create this bridge easily flowed into his consciousness.

The Rainbow Bridge manifested into form very quickly as he created it in the Quantum Field. In a short time, it was working to protect the Earth by bringing higher frequencies in, which intelligently identified, magnetized and transmuted the darker frequencies into the energies of Love.

Imukah continued to focus and added different codes into his machines, which created even higher, benevolent frequency transmissions flowing to the Earth Beings. He carefully programed the frequencies to affect Earth and it's different civilizations. It was always done with the intent for the highest, benevolent outcome. Although these energies were only directed to Earth, the entire Cosmos would benefit from the powerful transmutation of lower frequencies on Earth. Imukah was keenly aware of the connection between ALL; when one planet raises it's frequency, all planets benefit and are raised to a higher level as well.

Soon, the red alarm downgraded to orange and Imukah continued to strive for the green, all clear notice. There was still more to do, and he was up for the challenge.

After toning for quite some time, Sarah started to speak, *"Mahanaaaaaaaaaaaaaaaaaaa Godaheakaaaaaaaaaaaaaaaaaa*

Enahejaeeeeeeeeeeeeeeeeeeeeeeee! Mananehakoooooooooooooooohhhhhh! Edahatakaaaaaaaaaaaaaaaaaaaaaaaaaaaaaaaaa!"

Ronja added, *"Ochachdana machtadodacha Eschtanachoda Echa!"*

Kai joined in, *"Miimiimimimimi Mimimimi mmmiimmiiiiiimimiiiiiih!"*

Suddenly, Kai's energy shifted, and he started to speak "Dragon" in a loud and stern voice, *"Gonaheischteme. Natagohaida Edonamahaita Ebagaheschte Nadaheehschteme!"* As he spoke louder and louder, they all felt the vibration of these sounds flowing through their bodies.

Nina saw a lot of things during Kai's "Dragon" speech. She did not want to interrupt the flow of energies and decided to wait to share her visions at the end.

Ezrael kept his eyes closed to experience the meditation through feelings instead of activating his sight. He focused on enjoying and absorbing the frequencies. He sat next to his mother in a crossed legged meditation pose. His heart felt very open and he experienced energies circling intensely throughout his heart and his head. There was so much love and compassion flowing through his heart. He almost started to cry from this beautiful experience.

Suddenly, a Mountain Being appeared to Ronja in her mind's eye. He started to speak to her in a slow, deep voice, "Hello SumaRa. My name is Tartan. I am here to teach you how to create a specific Grid on Earth, and how to connect it to the Omniverse. You are part of 'the Emerald Green Soul Star Group', which has assisted all planets to ascend. You carry a specific code in your heart and you are just starting to remember how to activate it. All is done with love and compassion. I will be assisting you so you can do this work properly. You need to understand that this is a job that requires focus and pure intent. Do you want to work with me?" Tartan asked.

Ronja understood and of course was excited to work with this Mountain Being.

In the next moment, she was guided by Tartan to create a New Energy Matrix around the Earth. She was instructed to create this Matrix by sending focused 'love energy' out of her heart onto the planet. Ronja began sending love out to the Earth and soon saw many crystalline line structures rising up and out of Planet Earth, forming a grid pattern. This new energy grid expanded all the way around the whole planet. She lost her focus for a second and realized exactly during that time, that the energy grid was not created in a specific spot. Tartan was kind and patient with her, asked her to go back to the same spot and to send love out again. As she followed his instructions, the grid around the Earth was formed.

In the next moment, she saw a golden cord coming from her heart, connecting her to the new grid structure. The Mountain Being explained that she is now able to connect to the grid, whenever she feels guided, to send Love out from her heart.

Suddenly, a lot of energy flowed through Ronja. She started shaking and the Light Language came through, *"Edahada Manaheta Aka! Oooohhhhhhhhh Nonaheda Paka. Edagora odasoan nadaheda gobada!"*

She saw an emerald green color flowing into the newly formed Grid-Matrix. In this short period of time, the work was completed and her cord disconnected from the grid.

Tartan, the Mountain Being, thanked her and said, "For now, we are just going to focus on the energies for Earth. When you graduate from this work, we will expand the grid out to the Universe. After accomplishing this task, we will work with the grids of the Omniverse."

Ronja was very excited about this assignment and working with Tartan. Suddenly, the energy of the Mountain Being came through her. Ronja was guided to share the vibration of Tartan with the group. She spoke slowly in a very deep voice, *"Maaaaaaaaaaaaaaaaaaaaaneeeeeee eeeeeeeeeeeeeeeeaaaaaaaaaaaa, Akadehaaaaaaaaaaaaaaaaaanoooooooo, booooooomaaaaaaaaa."*

Nina was excited what she could see as Ronja spoke. She saw an energy grid being created around the Earth. She also saw energies coming out from the crystal grid which Kai had created. The energies from Kai's grid were flowing to different places on the planet. They continued their meditation for another few minutes.

Imukah was still working on the codes and suddenly the orange alarm turned into green and all was clear again. He felt relieved, while still working on the transmissions. He grinned and said, "Our Star Team is really starting to get a hang of working in the Quantum Field. And they do not even know how powerful they actually are. Now, because of their work today, the Earth is ready for me to transmit an even higher frequency."

Ammagant and Imero were very content with their successful deployment of Occuna's interference transmission. Imero, as promised, made the devices disappear and they both laughed and celebrated their imagined victory.

After a few minutes in silence, they closed their meditation circle with toning. Sarah thanked everyone and asked if anyone had experienced something they wanted to share.

Ronja shared about her experience with Tartan, the Mountain Being.

Kai shared about seeing his grid light up and energies going into electronic devices all over the planet. He also told the group about the help he had received from his dragon friends.

Ezrael shared what he felt in his body during the meditation and that he never had felt so peaceful in his whole life.

Sarah relayed about working with Dhalia, the Pleiadian Priestess, and Fiandra, the Sirian, her long time Guides from the Lemurian Council of the Cosmic Heart & Light.

Finally, it was Nina's turn and she was excited to share what she saw during the meditation. She told them about seeing energy coming from a sun like looking planet down to the Earth as a wave. She confirmed that she also saw different crystalline grids, some of them interconnecting with the trees. She saw that the roots of the trees were a a grid communication network as well. She also saw thousands of Dragons, Unicorns, Golden Dolphins and Whales returning to Earth through a beautiful rainbow. Nina had the "Inner Knowing" that these magical creatures were returning to help humanity. She could hear the heavenly sounds of these beings joyfully singing, and felt they were saying, "The New Earth is here".

She telepathically received the understanding that these Beings of Enchantment had left Earth due to the fall of Atlantis, a civilization from long time ago. They promised to return when the people of Earth would return back to love and start dreaming again. Because they felt the pure love of this Lemurian Star Team and their innocence, they knew it was time to fulfill their promise.

All were excited to hear what everyone had to share. Their first conference call meditation was a great experience and they could not wait to call in again at 6 am the next morning.

Merlin and Novix smiled at each other, and Novix said, "Master, they did it again. I am astonished by their powerful work."

Merlin looked at him with a smile and replied, "Wait until you see what will happen, when all humans wake up to their multidimensional Higher Selves and find their divine spark within. We will see a planet like nowhere else before!"

Novix replied, "I am looking forward to seeing this myself, Master. And, as you know, the dark forces will not give up easily."

Merlin explained, "Well, let us see, Novix! We are ready to support them whenever we are needed. Dark versus light had been the game since the beginning of time, and light and love will always transform the dark! You know that, Novix, and sometimes it needs to get dark before we totally embrace the light. In the end, when the humans finally find God within, the game is over. Everything is always benevolent, always in alignment with the Creator to evolve consciousness. I am excited to see what will happen next. I see the potentials and what I see is beautiful!"

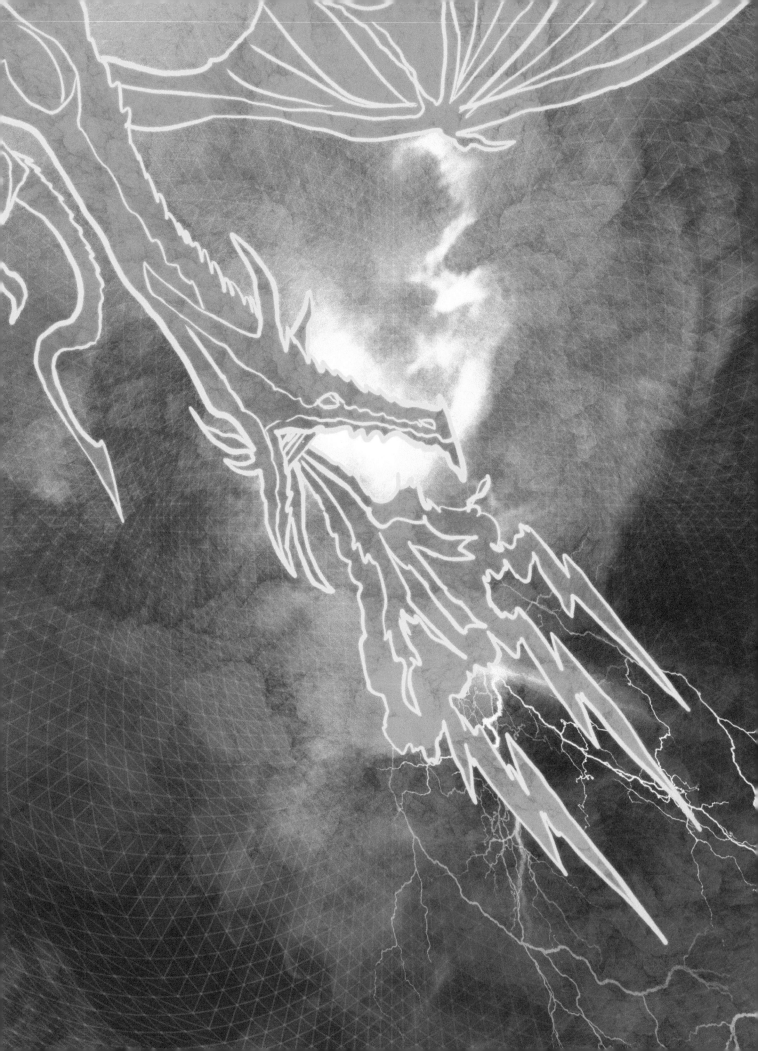

CHAPTER 13

The Clearing

Sarah and Ezrael were eating breakfast together after their first meditation call. Both felt so much bliss and gratitude in their hearts.

Sarah received another text from Todd with a request to visit Ezrael. Todd had promised Sarah, that he would not reach out to Ezrael directly until she felt he was fully recovered.

Todd was wondering how his friend Ezrael was doing. He had not talked to Ezrael since the incident at the waterfall, a few days back, and felt somehow guilty about what had happened to his best friend.

Todd was anxious to talk to Ezrael to find out what really happened that day. He could only remember that he picked up breakfast for Ezrael and himself, walked towards the waterfall and he remembered a strong wind gust. After that was a blank until he woke up in the hospital with his parents by his side. It was quite a shock for all of them, and especially finding out Ezrael was getting worse.

Sarah read Todd's text, thought for a while, and then asked Ezrael, "Todd reached out again and would like to meet with you. What do you think about that, Ezrael?"

Ezrael replied, "Well, I guess it is time. We have been best friends for so many years. I still feel a little bit uncomfortable about seeing him. I do not want to judge or blame him, but I feel he had something to do with me landing in the hospital. However, I am ready to find out more."

Sarah replied, "Let us not assume anything, Ezrael. He is your best friend and he would never intentionally harm you. You know that. Every experience we have in our lives is for our highest good. We are living in new times, Ezrael. This morning, I received a new perspective from my Pleiadian Guide, that there is no Karma. All is based on the Law of Attraction."

"What do you mean, Mom?" Ezrael asked with curiosity.

Sarah looked at Ezrael and replied, "Everything that comes to us is based on the law of attraction. Meaning when you continuously vibrate on a lower frequency, you will attract suffering and create a vicious circle. The good news is, that the new energies are here to help us all to clear so we can vibrate on a higher frequency. We just have to unlearn everything we have ever learned and create new pathways in our brain to allow new perspectives and positive thoughts. It is our job to stop old programming that keeps us believing everything will always happen the same way as it did before.

For example, when we go through something difficult, we could see it as an opportunity to practice changing our thought patterns and always expect the most benevolent outcome ever."

Sarah continued to explain, "Before, we were all on a path of healing, striving for wholeness. In the new energies we are remembering our Divinity, that we are already whole and complete. We can finally feel God within us, experience unconditional love and compassion for ourselves and others. It is only when we are in that space of love, that we can see the beauty and benevolence of life. Higher DNA frequencies help us with that shift of perspective. When we consistently vibrate on a higher frequency, love ourselves, we attract magic to us. There is only love, we all are Divine and come from Oneness. You have an opportunity right now to find compassion and forgiveness for Todd. I am inviting you to make this an opportunity to work with the higher vibrational frequencies of love."

Sarah paused for a while, and then continued, "Todd was a conduit for something or someone, Ezrael. Without this experience with Todd, I feel, you would not be where you are now. If you look at life from above the veil, every soul is innocent and there is only love. Every soul is here to help all other souls grow. We love each other so much and are all cheering for each other to evolve and to finally get it. It is all about a shift in perspective. When we remember who we truly are, then life becomes art, and we can finally create together. Love, compassion, kindness and forgiveness are the keys for our evolution. Does this make sense?"

Ezrael replied, "I guess it all does make sense. We just need to learn how to use these new energies and believe that all is already here. We have to learn to be in the 'Now', without filtering in our old stories."

"Yes, Ezrael, you got it," Sarah laughed. "Why don't you text Todd and ask him to come by for a visit this morning? I will be home and we could see him together. What do you think about that?"

Ezrael replied, "I think this is a good idea. I still do not want to text him though. Mom, can you just text him for me?"

"Yes, Ezrael," Sarah replied, "Would 10 am work for you today?"

Ezrael agreed and Sarah texted Todd to see if he was free. Todd responded 'yes' immediately. He was eager to see his best friend again and to find out more about that strange day.

Ezrael felt a little anxious and restless as he waited for Todd to arrive. He wished he could remember more about what happened to him at the waterfall.

Todd was nervous as he walked to Ezrael's house. As he arrived at their place, Sarah welcomed him with a big smile and hugged him. He immediately felt more at ease and very relieved.

Ezrael was waiting for him in the living room and the boys greeted each other. Both were still a little nervous. Sarah had lit a candle and incense was burning as usual. Today, she was also guided to burn some sage for clearing. She brought Todd something to drink and then they all sat down together.

Ezrael observed Todd with his new sight. Interestingly enough, he did not see gold, nor silver and hardly any symbols around Todd. The symbols that he did see were not flowing properly, almost as if they were sticking together in his energy field. All of Todd's chakras did not seem to flow properly either and there was a lot of gray energy around his head area. Also, the color in his heart area was not emerald green, as he had been seeing with his mom and all his new-found friends. Todd's color was a grass green combined with gray. When he glanced at Todd's phone, he saw black energy around it. Ezrael was concerned about what he just saw but did not know what to do just yet.

Ammagant and Imero, still in Imero's study, were in high spirits after successful deployment of Occuna's Interference transmission. The battery station was back up to 90% and life was good again.

Suddenly Ammagant got excited and said to Imero, "Our boy, Imero! Our boy! I feel him. He is with the Chosen One at the moment."

"What do you mean?" Imero asked.

Ammagant replied, "Do you remember the Chosen One's best friend, Todd, or whatever his name was? The one I connected you with, so you could take over his body and fight this Ezrael boy? I do not even want to pronounce his name, as it gives me chills and it disgusts me!"

"Of course I remember," Imero said, waiting to hear more.

"I can still trace this boy, as I might have forgotten to mention. I continued to infuse him with dark energies during his night sleep and that is how I can continue to trace him. At the moment, our boy is together with this Chosen One," Ammagant explained.

Imero looked at Ammagant with excitement and said, "This is exciting! Let me think quickly about what we can do!"

As both boys seemed to be very uncomfortable, Sarah started the conversation, "You both went through a very scary experience and I am so glad that both of you are okay, which is the most important thing."

Sarah asked Todd, "How are you doing and could you please tell us what you remember?"

Todd answered, "I have been tired since the event at the waterfall and I am not sure why. I have been feeling very down and have had low energy. I am also having nightmares every night, where I am drowning in dark matter, almost like I am out in the Cosmos and getting sucked into a dark hole. Every morning I have been waking up with a feeling of despair."

Ezrael and Sarah listened attentively as Todd continued, "I only remember stopping to buy breakfast for us. When I was on the way to the waterfall, a huge gust of wind kicked up a sand storm. Everything went black in front of my eyes. The next thing I remember is waking up in the hospital. What happened in between is a mystery to me."

Ezrael became irritated and said, "I remember you coming to the waterfall and you were acting very strange. It seemed like somebody else was within you. I felt pain everywhere in my body and collapsed to the ground as you came near me. You kneeled next to me and said that you were Imero and that I needed to look into your eyes, which I did. I felt a darkness in your eyes. Somehow, I thought that I could withstand your stare, and I did for a while. It was when you said something that made me doubt myself, that I lost and went unconscious."

Sarah said to Ezrael, "Well, you might think you lost but I do believe that in the end you actually won. Your spirit continued to do the work during your coma state and I truly believe that you have won that battle. Think about it Ezrael, you said when you woke up in the hospital something had shifted for you, and I believe you shifted something for the world too."

Ezrael replied, "Well, Mom…Yes, something has shifted for me, but I do not want to make it a bigger deal than it is."

Ammagant said to Imero, "Todd and this boy Ezrael are together at the moment with Ezrael's mom. I can still trace our boy, through his lower vibrational energies. My concern is though, if he spends too much time with these Lemurians, it might change, and I won't be able to trace him anymore."

Imero eagerly replied, "Maybe it is time to send him some dark energies and orders? Can you do this, Ammagant?"

"Master, I will try to reach him," Ammagant replied and started sending all his dark energy to Todd.

Suddenly, Todd was not feeling well. He started shaking and Ezrael was shocked as he saw dark energies flowing into Todd and creating a black cloud around him.

Ezrael started screaming, "Mom, we need to do something right now!!! Todd needs our help! There are dark energies all around him. Do something!"

Sarah very calmly said to Ezrael, "Let us sit on the floor and put Todd in between us and hold hands around him."

After they positioned themselves, Sarah said, "Let us tone, Ezrael."

They closed their eyes and started toning together, *"AAAAAAAHHHHHHHHHHHHHHHHHHHHH-HHHHH."*

Suddenly, it came to Sarah to tell Ezrael to keep his eyes open. So he did. Sarah took a few deep breaths and said, "We call in Buddha Ganesh to transmute these energies, to amplify the 'love energy', and to bring in peace. We call in Archangel Michael, Merlin, the Lemurian Council of the Cosmic Heart & Light, our Higher Selves and all the benevolent, highest vibrational Cosmic Beings, who want to be with us Right Here and Right Now!"

Ezrael was surprised to see all these Cosmic Beings of Light, which his mom just called in, appear instantly. He was in awe when he saw a huge white, large Elephant as well as many different Cosmic Light Beings surrounding them in a circle. Ezrael also saw white and golden energies coming into the circle from these Light Beings around them. For the first time, he could hear them as well. He heard them all humming together with a *"MMMMMMMMMMMMMHHHHHHHHHHHHH"* sound.

Although Sarah had her eyes closed she started to sing the same sound as the Intergalactic Beings of Light, *"MMMMMMMMMHHHHHHHHH."*

Ezrael soon joined her.

Sarah started speaking in a very stern voice, *"Aktogoda Namagata Etafaria Onaheate matanora ehamanahata aka. MMMMMMMMMMhhhh!"*

As Sarah spoke, Ezrael saw the energies shifting. At the same time, he also saw Merlin fly in with a magic wand and disconnected the dark energies from Todd. He saw a purple dragon spitting energetic fire on Todd and finally the dark cloud disappeared.

Todd still had his eyes closed and was shaking, but he finally felt more comfortable.

Meanwhile, back at Imero's study, Ammagant was still focusing on Todd.

Imero started to get impatient and asked, "What is going on? Tell me Ammagant!"

Ammagant, still concentrating, started shaking as well and just quickly said to Imero, "Give me a moment. I am doing something here!"

Suddenly, as Ezrael and Sarah continued to hum with the Cosmic Light Beings, Ezrael saw a version of himself coming in! He saw himself right in front of Todd, riding on a large, red dragon. He could not believe his eyes and was guided to hum even louder.

Suddenly, the other Ezrael looked sternly into Ezrael's eyes and commanded, "SPEAK!" while the red dragon blew energetic fire on Ezrael. Ezrael had to close his eyes as he felt intense energies flowing into his body and spoke in the Cosmic Language of Light for the first time, in a very deep voice, *"MACHTAGURDA ECHTOAHEDA MADANORAGA ECHTOGADIA EMANEHA GODENABETA!"*

Sarah, still keeping her eyes closed, had to grin, full of excitement. She thought to herself, "It is happening! It is happening! Oh my God! He is starting to remember and he is connecting with his multidimensional, cosmic Higher Self. Ezrael is starting to gain access to his powers!"

Ezrael felt something come over him, he started to shake as well. His voice became even stronger and this time, he felt as if he was speaking for his dragon, *"Choschtaaaaaaaaaaaaaaaaaaaahhhhhhhhhhhhhhh! Mechtakadaaaaaaaaaaahhhhhhhh! Bechtanahaaaaaaaaahhhhhhhhhhh!"*

Ezrael opened his eyes and was stunned by what he saw. Before his eyes, were golden symbols which were flowing into Todd. They were floating and spinning in his energy field. Next, he saw all of Todd's chakras opening, with white light spinning and radiating out in a clockwise manner. Shortly after, he noticed that all the sticky symbols were gone.

To his great surprise, when he looked at his mom, he saw her as a blue Avatar. He could not believe what he was seeing. She had her eyes closed. A huge, dark purple dragon, along with many other Cosmic Beings of Light, were standing right behind her. He recognized a number of them because they had been present at the last meditation call.

Sarah, still in the blue Avatar form, started speaking in a very gentle voice, *"MmmmmmmmmmmmmmmmmmmmmH-hhhhhhhhhhhhhhhhhhhhhhhhhh. Dddddddddddd dddd ddd dddd dddddd dddddd ddd dddd dddddddddd,*

Mimimiimimimi mmmimimimimii mimmimmi mimimimimimimmiiii."

While she was speaking, Ezrael saw the emerald green energy flow from her heart into Todd's heart, transforming the grass green and grayish colors surrounding his heart into the same emerald green color as hers. Also, he saw the golden-silver strand from his mom being duplicated and transferred into Todd. Next, he saw a large, beautiful Light Being taking an object out of the back of Todd's neck, which looked like a computer chip. He did not know that this Cosmic Light Being was Dhalia, his mom's Guide. He could sense her benevolence, her high frequency and her unconditional love.

While his mom was still chanting, *"Mmmmmmmhhhhhhhhhhhhhhhhh,"* Dhalia suddenly stared directly into Ezrael's eyes and said, "Welcome home, Lazumar! Welcome home! You are finally back. Nothing will ever be the same. You are starting to remember! You are one of us!"

As his mom continued to chant, her voice became louder and stronger and shifted from a low vibration to a very high-pitched sound, *"MMMMMMMMmmmimimimimimimiiiiihhiimimimiiiiiiiiiimmimimi!"*

Suddenly, Ezrael saw an explosion of white light bursting out from Todd's body into the room. Sarah stopped speaking, opened her eyes and everything was over. All the Cosmic Beings of Light, the other Light Beings and Buddha Ganesh were gone.

Ammagant started screaming, "NOOOOOOOOO! They have done it again. Those Lemurian Monsters!"

Imero screamed in reply, "Ammagant what is going on? Tell me now!"

"We lost Todd. He is out of the Matrix now! We have lost him," Ammagant said in an angry voice.

"Are you telling me we just got defeated by two little humans?" Imero yelled in disbelief.

"No, Master, we were defeated by two Lemurian Masters, accessing the Quantum Field with their Intergalactic Helpers," Ammagant responded.

Suddenly, they received a telepathic report that the battery charging station had dropped down to 50%.

Todd opened his eyes and was breathing normally again and said, "I do not know what you guys just did, but I feel really good now. Thank you so much!"

Todd looked at Ezrael and continued, "I am sorry for whatever I did, Ezrael. Please trust me it was never my intention to harm you." Todd felt so much love and compassion in his heart and he started to feel tears filling his eyes. He could not remember when he had cried last.

"No worries, Todd," Ezrael replied with a smile, "You might have helped me more than you think!"

Todd gave both of them a hug and said, "This was the weirdest thing that ever happened to me. If I did not know you two so well, I would have called 911 to get you both admitted to a psychiatric ward."

They all started laughing and their laughter was so joyous and contagious, they did not know how to stop.

Sarah put her hands onto Todd's shoulders and looked straight into his eyes and said, "It was not you, Todd. From today on, nothing like this can ever happen to you again. We do not need to understand everything that happened. But let us see it in the positive way. Because of the event at the waterfall, you are here today. Ezrael would not have found his power. It is all perfect. It is all divine and now we can co-create in a different manner. When we are out of the Matrix, the fun actually starts."

Todd was not really in a mental state of comprehending what Sarah had just said. He never heard of the Matrix before. At the moment, Todd was just glad that he felt better and everything seemed to be resolved with his best friend.

Ezrael asked Todd to show him his cell phone and smiled when he saw all white light around Todd's phone.

"Mom, we are doing great work here. You are right. We do not need to know exactly what we are actually doing. But it is nice to see results," Ezrael said and laughed.

"Yes, Ezrael, we just need to trust and call in the highest, benevolent forces and surrender. Welcome home, Ezrael! You have integrated some of your Lemurian magic today with the help of your Higher Self, your powerful Dragon and my Guide, Dhalia. And, welcome home to you too, Todd!"

Ezrael was struck by what his mom just said. Was it possible that she was in the same space as he had been? Was it possible that she had seen the same Light Beings as he did? He could not wait to ask her more questions and wanted to wait until Todd left.

Sarah looked at Ezrael and said, "I feel like it is time for you to rest again."

Then she looked at Todd and said, "We are going to hold a ceremony on the Full Moon and we would love to have you join us."

Todd was excited about this and agreed. He had so many more questions about what just happened. He was so curious to find out what that strange language was, but he knew it was not the right time to ask.

Sarah also invited him to the light language meditation calls and he was intrigued by this as well. Something magical just happened to him. The only thing he felt inside of him at this moment was love and bliss. He was willing to explore these mysteries further.

After Sarah shared the meditation phone number with Todd, he needed to leave. All said goodbye to each other, and off he went to his soccer practice, never feeling better in his whole life. He felt powerful, full of love, and free.

CHAPTER 14

The Grand Plan

Imero and Ammagant were still very upset about their little defeat on the first day of the Transmission. Thankfully, Occuna had explained that it would take two weeks until the infiltration would be totally established. Over the last couple of days, the transmissions were working well to keep the lower energies on the planet alive. Imero felt a little bit stronger again, as the battery charging station suddenly went back up to 70%. There was still hope.

Since the implementation of the dark force's transmission by Imero, more fear was felt on Planet Earth. The humans struggled with increased anger issues and despair. Many felt hopeless, not seeing a way out of the repeated trauma cycles and suffering. The humans did not realize that every time they watched TV, talked on the phone or played games on their tablets, the dark energies were filtering into their pineal gland and calcifying it. They were becoming more susceptible to Imero's mind controlling thoughts through the Matrix.

The humans were not even aware that anything was different as they were so used to fear and feeling separated from all there is. Sadly, it was normal for them to experience increased fear states and struggle.

Thankfully, these low vibrational energies were not affecting all the humans. The humans on Planet Earth, who had already activated their DNA to a higher frequency, were only minimally impacted. Plus, there were many other Starseed groups on the planet, uniting and doing work to counteract the impact of the dark's transmissions. The Star Team's light language meditation calls were having a powerful impact as well, although they were not fully aware of how they had tremendously shifted the energies on Earth. They were Lemurian Masters working in the Quantum Field.

Imero knew something else needed to be done now, before the Solar Eclipse. He was aware that the Full Moon always weakened his Matrix, because the ceremonies held by humans around the planet during this time, counteracted his dark transmissions. The Full Moon was only a day away.

Suddenly, Imero received a telepathic message from Kamit, who was the Reptilian spokesperson for 'the Gedoha Clan'. He emphasized to Imero that something bigger needed to be done now. Imero knew what to do.

Imero decided to reach out to Occuna again. Although he did not like to admit that he needed help, he remembered what was discussed at the last Inner Earth Meeting. It was made clear that he needed to work with Occuna and make sure he stayed happy and working for their side. Imero decided to forget about his pride for a while.

Imero went towards a small table in his study where a black crystal was lying. This crystal, while holding it, connected him instantly with Occuna and made him appear by pure intent. Imero picked up the crystal and closed his eyes to call in Occuna.

Sarah, Ezrael, Ronja, Nina and Kai continued to connect during the daily morning meditation calls over the next few days. Todd joined a couple of the calls, but due to his summer work it was not always possible for him to attend so early in the morning.

The group started to feel very connected with each other. They received specific homework instructions while working with the Light Beings during the calls. Yes, they connected with the Lemurian Council of the Cosmic Heart & Light, Buddha Ganesh and many other Ascended Masters. The team received their guidance through their mind's eye as they meditated together each day at 6 am.

Sarah's main focus was to organize the first Light Language Ceremony, which was coming up tomorrow for the Full Moon. She also invited several of her friends who spoke Light Language. Some of them were guided to ask their children, teens who were in Ezrael's age group, to attend as well.

Sarah, who up to this time, had held monthly Peruvian Fire Full Moon and Medicine Wheel Ceremonies, received guidance to shift her focus to Light Language Ceremonies. It was important to bring in higher cosmic frequencies onto the planet. She knew it was time to merge the Cosmic energies with the Earth energies in a different way.

Imero felt a blast of wind and in the next moment, Occuna appeared. He was thankful to see Occuna and bowed his head, just to show some respect, and said, "Dear great Occuna! I want to thank you for this transmission device! It works wonderfully on Earth. My energy has increased since then and the Inner Earth battery charging station has increased to 70% and seems to be holding strong. Of course, we want to see it back up to 100% or above."

Occuna responded, "I agree! I am benefitting from these powerful forces as well. These energies also radiate out into the Omniverse. Do not think that I created these devices to only impact the Earth."

Occuna paused and suddenly laughed out loud and continued, "Yes, these energies feed me even more than you. I am the Dark Emperor of the Galaxies, and you must know that I do everything to serve myself. The energies you are receiving are nothing compared to the power which I am receiving!" Occuna continued to laugh while Imero felt Occuna's powerful dark presence.

Imero started visualizing himself as the Dark Emperor of the Galaxies and was wondering how he could become the most powerful dark force in the Omniverse. He decided to play along and said to Occuna, "Yes, Occuna, you are the most powerful dark force in the Galaxies. Thank you for helping us and we are wondering if you could help us further?"

Occuna asked, "What do you need?"

Imero continued, "We are entering a very powerful time on Earth. Tomorrow is the Full Moon and two days later is the Solar Eclipse. As you know, the positive energies on Earth will increase. I am not taking anything lightly anymore as I am aware that the Lemurians have started to unite and use their powers collectively and quantumly. We need your help again to send some energies to Earth to counteract these events."

"I am already taking care of it," Occuna responded, "I have created a specific energy transmission device that can only be used here on Earth during the Solar Eclipse. I was wondering if you, Imero, could take on this important task and operate my new device? I cannot be here when it happens, as I have to oversee everything from my secret power station."

Imero, filled with excitement, agreed to this task. He was grateful to have a chance to gain even more power soon. But Occuna was not done…

"You know, I am the Grand Master of the Galaxies," Occuna continued, "and I am doing you a very big favor to keep you in power."

Imero had to agree and said, "Yes, Master! What do you need in return?"

Occuna started to grin and said, "I want you, Imero, to give up your rights as the Emperor of Darkness here on Earth. You have done well enough, but it seems you do not have the power anymore to help with the increase of the dark forces. I am going to give Ammagant the position, as he is shifting his energies tremendously through my presence."

Imero was shocked to hear this news, became irritated and said, "Occuna, you cannot do this to me. I have worked hard for thousands of years to support the dark forces on Earth. You cannot get rid of me just like that! You know I have powers beyond your capacity, if you just give me another chance and let me show you what I am capable of. I am the dark Master Magician of Earth and I have invented the Matrix which has helped you as well. I want you to give me another chance, Occuna!"

Occuna looked at him and said sternly, "Alright, Imero! I am giving you one more chance. If you fulfill my task in a perfect manner during the Solar Eclipse, you shall stay here and keep some powers. But you need to understand that I am taking over Earth as we speak. You will not have the same rights anymore. From now on, I will be the Emperor of the Dark Forces on Earth as well. You could possibly become my disciple, if you wish to surrender and accept your new downgraded position. Otherwise, you will need to leave and find a place in the Galaxy to start anew."

Imero was shocked and speechless about what Occuna's had just said. The remembrance of the Inner Earth Meeting returned in his mind and he recalled how Kamit suggested that he needed to listen to Occuna and follow his suggestions. Imero now wondered if Kamit knew about what Occuna had planned all along.

Imero, feeling in the moment that he had no other choice, said, "Dearest Occuna, I am in total service to you. I do not wish to leave this planet and I am willing to serve you. You are the Dark Emperor of the Galaxies! And I am willing to surrender and will fulfill your task in the best manner. Just trust me! Thank you!" Imero said, trying his best to sound enthusiastic.

Occuna warned Imero, "Well, I have worked with the Dark Emperors of other planets before. It has been my experience that Emperors have the hardest time letting go of their position and power. A lot of times, they had to leave in the end anyway. It was much easier for me to work with the disciples of the Emperors. Maybe you will show me something new. I am willing to work with you, Imero. But trust me, I will know if you are on the way to regain full power again. If I even sense this is happening, you will be teleported out within a split second and you will not have a chance of ever returning to Earth. I oversee and know everything, Imero. I have known about what will happen on Earth before you were ever involved. Do not underestimate me, Imero! As I said, I am giving you one chance. If you mess it up, you are out!"

Imero nodded his head and said, "Master, I won't disappoint you. I will do my work during the Solar Eclipse and you will be proud of me."

Occuna responded, "I do not need to be proud of my disciples. I only need to be proud of myself and my creations, because I am the ONE who is the creator of it all."

The Dark Emperor of the Galaxies made a black square box appear and gave it to Imero. This is my new device and you will use it exactly for the few minutes during the Solar Eclipse, when we are at the darkest minutes. Is that clear? I will watch you from afar and will give you telepathic instructions, if I feel you need my help. The shift to increase the dark is now in your hands. Do not mess it up," Occuna stated.

In a split second, Occuna disappeared.

CHAPTER 15

The Preparation

Sarah was cleaning up the backyard to prepare for the next day's first Light Language Ceremony, when Ezrael came outside to join her. He had just talked to his father, as he did every day, to give him an update on how he was doing. A few days back, they all had a very nice dinner together. However, he and his mom did not share anything about their spiritual adventures.

Ezrael continued to enjoy his new sight and realized more and more what a gift it was. With his new ability he saw exactly what was going on energetically with the people on Earth in every moment. Recently, he started to understand what the different colors and symbols represented. In the last few days, he witnessed color changes around people, which he had not seen before. He started to see gray and black appearing around people's heads and hearts, as well as black energy around cell phones and other electronic devices.

He had not seen any changes around his mom until today. He saw dark energies trying to enter her energy field. Somehow though, it seemed that this black energy was bouncing off of her, but he noticed some dark energies lingering around her pineal gland. He wondered what that was all about and decided to observe, rather than to share with anyone.

Sarah smiled at her son and said, "Hello, Love! Are you ready and as excited as I am about tomorrow?"

"Yes, Mom, I am very excited. I am already feeling high and benevolent energies coming into the space. I see golden and silver energies already around the fire pit and white pillars of light, eight of them, surrounding the ceremony area. These energies were not here yesterday, and I am sensing they came in because you are cleaning up the yard," Ezrael said.

"That is how it works," Sarah replied, "We cannot underestimate what we are actually doing energetically, when we allow ourselves to be fully present with an open heart. This is called alignment, and it is the magic of our multidimensional work."

Ezrael was intrigued by her statement and asked, "What do you mean?"

Sarah replied, "When we are fully present we have access to all dimensions simultaneously. The trick is to bypass the mind and it's chatter. Meditation has really helped me with clearing my mind and staying present in my heart. With practice, meditation can be done in every moment and through every activity in our lives. That is the new paradigm."

Ezrael asked, "Mom, can you tell me more about the remembering process?"

Sarah paused for a moment and replied, "Remembering is a natural process and cannot be forced. When we have the intention to remember, we start to receive insights about our multidimensional Higher Selves, almost like pieces of a puzzle. Sometimes it makes sense, and sometimes it does not, until another piece comes in, and then all of a sudden it makes sense again. I do not know if we ever fully complete the puzzle in one lifetime. I do know we receive the pieces we need, exactly when we need them. We are all in different stages of remembering and different stages of consciousness. We are all equal no matter what stage we are in. It is not about how much you know and remember about yourself, it is about how you act in the world. A true master is kind, compassionate and loving to every being, in every moment. The remembering process can sometimes be very intense, as it was for me." Sarah became quiet and was suddenly deep in thought.

"Mom, tell me more! What do you mean?" Ezrael asked.

Sarah and Ezrael sat down in lawn chairs and Sarah said, "My remembering started when I attended a Light Language Ceremony, a long time ago. I did not know what this ceremony was all about, but I knew I had to attend. You know how this works, Ezrael…"

She smiled at him and continued, "After that event, I started to speak Light Language to the cats, the plants, in the car… It just came through when it came through. At first, I kept it to myself, because it seemed very strange to me and I did not want to be judged as crazy. I continued to attend different kinds of ceremonies and met many people like me, who were also speaking the Cosmic Language of Light, and some were not even aware of what it was until I shared. However, speaking Light Language was activating my pineal gland and strengthened my connection to my higher multidimensional self. My Guides then changed to Cosmic Guides and I started working with the Pleiadians and the Sirians, who also embody the Lemurian energies. When I speak the Language of Light, somehow it gets me out of my linear mind and connects me directly to my heart and Oneness. Little by little, I gained insights about many of my past lives. As we spend more time in the space of quantum, there is no time, and all lives are happening simultaneously. So, is there really a past?"

Ezrael, a little frustrated, trying to understand what his mom was talking about, said, "This is getting a little complicated now. Can you just tell me what you remember in simple terms?"

Sarah laughed and continued to share, "I started to remember Lemuria. In some of these lives, I worked with plants and facilitated ceremonies, which helped people develop their telepathic abilities further. All my friends in Lemuria worked on different kinds of DNA activations as well. I have been blessed to meet some of them in this life again. We knew that Lemuria had to fall, it was part of the Divine Plan. We established mind frequencies that would allow us to communicate without being traced or detected and we were able to share important information which helped us to leave at the right time. We went to different star systems to continue our work. I became a Diplomat and traveled to different star systems. That's why I am able to speak many different Languages of Light. When I visited several different powerful places on Earth, it activated my remembering process even further, as I discovered I had lived some of my Lemurian lives in these locations."

Sarah, who rarely shared these experiences with others, was excited and so grateful to have this bond with her son.

She continued, "In another life in Lemuria, I was a historian and was the keeper and protector of the ancient teachings of the Stars. I loved the stories and treasured them very much. Now it is time to bring them forth in this lifetime, to help to bring the energies of Lemuria back."

Ezrael asked, "How do you want to do this, Mom?"

Sarah replied, "Besides starting to hold Light Language Ceremonies, which will help to activate this remembering in others, I am going to start writing stories about the ancient teachings of the Stars. I recently started writing. Spirit wakes me up at 3:33 am almost every morning. I get up, listen and start writing. All I do is surrender and the words flow. We all are channels and receive messages from the Stars or our Higher Selves. We just think that we are doing it, although, it is often channelled material.

"Mom, this sounds very exciting," Ezrael replied. "But what can I do to start remembering? Mom, I want to remember!"

Sarah answered, "The meditation calls are already activating your DNA. The upcoming ceremonies will activate you even further. Just trust, Ezrael. Sometimes there is interference from the dark side and lower vibrational beings can come through, but this is nothing truly to be concerned about. As long as your heart is pure, you have strong intent to be of service for the Cosmos and call in the highest frequencies of benevolence, your discernment will be strong. love and light will always transmute the dark. You are already on the fast track, Ezrael. So much has opened up for you in the last few days. Enjoy the journey that Spirit has in store for you, stay in the moment and trust. Sometimes reading a book will activate you or talking to another person…there are many ways to do so."

After a pause, Sarah continued, "Even when you remember your powerful, multidimensional Higher Self, you cannot be attached to any part of your identity. You are more advanced on this journey than most others you will meet, so you could flatter yourself about who you are. The real treasure when you find the divine within you is to share love, compassion and kindness with the world. For me, it is about being everything and nothing at the same time. It is important to activate as many people as possible and then support them in freeing themselves from the Matrix…The Matrix of Illusion."

"What do you mean by the Matrix of Illusion, Mom?" Ezrael asked.

"The Matrix is a frequency of mind control which keeps us stuck in fear and separation. It prevents us from feeling and seeing who we truly are; part of Mother/Father God. The Matrix keeps us on a lower vibratory DNA frequency. It creates the illusion to believe that everything is outside of us, instead of within and only outside influences can make us happy."

"How do people know if they are out of the Matrix?" Ezrael asked.

Sarah smiled and replied, "Great question, Ezrael. Let me see if I can give you a decent answer... You start feeling the Divinity within yourself, and love and compassion start to override fear. You start seeing the world as beautiful and benevolent. Critical and outside of the box thinking becomes natural and you start to question everything. You are no longer willing to conform and blindly follow rules or authority figures which are out of integrity. You start seeing the divine magic in others and you feel the intense urge to unite with a like-minded community to serve the light. Another sign is that you start connecting with your body on a higher level. The body starts responding to your demands and positive thoughts. When you release the old template of needing to die to remember, you start to remember even further. Even if people are struggling all around you, when you are awake, you can hold the light for others with love and compassion without participating in their suffering."

Ezrael said, "This is exactly what has happened to me since I woke up. I feel so much lighter and happier than ever before. Thank you so much for your insights and sharing, Mom. It really helped."

Sarah, feeling such joy and connection with her son, replied, "Thank you so much for being curious and listening to my story. I have not shared it with anyone for a while. It feels good being listened to. Also, Ezrael, it is important for you to understand, that your generation of children are already more advanced than we were at your age. Most children, being born now, are already out of the Matrix due to their highly activated DNA structure. They are blessed to come in remembering. They do not have to go through this kind of amnesia to remember who they are, to get to the light. I truly believe that this is the last lifetime we have to do it this way."

Sarah paused for a while and then said, "I would love to talk to you further, but it is time for me to get back to work."

Ezrael stayed and helped his mom with the preparation for the ceremony. Suddenly, he saw black energies entering his moms auric field. He did not know what to do.

In the same moment, Sarah said, "Wow, I feel a little dizzy. I think I need to go inside and rest for a while."

Ezrael, very concerned, said, "Let me walk you inside and I will bring you a glass of water. I will help you, everything will get done by tomorrow. I need to go out and do a few things, so you rest for a while and I will pick up dinner on my way back. What do you think?"

Sarah looked at him with a tired smile and replied, "Ezrael, this sounds perfect. Thank you!"

Ezrael helped his mom into the house, brought her water and left. He immediately texted all his new friends, "We need to meet NOW, ASAP! Where can we meet?"

Ronja texted back right away and said it was okay to meet at her house. Kai, Nina and Todd all sensed an urgency and just left what they were doing and headed to Ronja's house.

Ezrael practically ran the whole way to their meeting place. His heart was pounding and he started to remember his discussion with his mom. Instead of falling into fear, he decided to connect with his heart and he started calling in all the benevolent Light Beings for his mom. He trusted his instinct to call in his friends, and started to smile as he heard himself say, "One for all! All for One!"

CHAPTER 16

The Emergency Meeting

Ronja was curious about the urgent meeting called by Ezrael. She smudged her bedroom, lit candles and, burned incense. Ronja was guided to place her crystal singing bowls into the center of the room. All of them showed up on time. Kai brought his crystals and created a grid near Ronja's bowls. He just knew what to do and everyone was excited about being together. Todd arrived as well and was introduced by Ezrael to the rest of the group. All were excited to have another member in their soul tribe.

They all sat down in a circle and Kai said, "Thank you Ezrael for getting us together and Ronja for opening your space for us. I am really glad you did, as I felt an urgency to unite with you guys in person today too."

Ezrael said, "Yes, me too. I cannot explain what is happening. For a few days now, I see gray and black cloudy energy around people's heads and on their cell phones. To my greatest concern though, I just saw dark energies coming into my mom. That is why I called you all together. I was helping prepare for tomorrow's ceremony, when I saw the dark energies working their way into her body and she said she felt so tired that she needed to rest. I texted you right away because I felt there was something we could do together to help my mom. Thank you for showing up on such short notice. Are you willing to help me?"

Meanwhile, Sarah did not go to bed. She knew what needed to be done. Sarah went into her healing room instead, created sacred space, sat down on the floor and started to meditate.

They all agreed and were willing to be of service as usual. Kai said that he was not surprised that Sarah was targeted, as she was the facilitator for tomorrow's ceremony.

As this was the first time Todd was meeting with the group, he said, "I am not really sure what I am doing here, but I want to help with the best of my ability."

Ezrael replied, "Thank you, friend, this means a lot to me. Your pure intention to be of service is most important. All you need to do is stay present."

Ronja said, "Before we start, we need to put Sarah into the center and ask her spirit for permission to receive support from us."

Ezrael said, "This is a good idea. I did not even think about that."

Next, they all closed their eyes, except for Ezrael. He was relieved to see that his friends' energy fields were all clear. While all closed their eyes and focused on Sarah's essence being in the middle of their circle, Ezrael saw his mom coming in as well. To his surprise, his mom looked like the blue Avatar again. She appeared to be so wise, powerful and strong. She looked at him with a smile and winked, as if she knew what was going on. Then she nodded her head, in agreement to the session they intended to do to help her. All the others intuitively received the same message. She was open to receive.

At the same time, Sarah, back in her healing room, had connected with them telepathically and gave permission for them to work with her. Yes, she was fully aware of what was going on.

All of them held hands in a circle and started to tone together three times, *"AAAAAAAAAAAAAAAAAAHHHHHHHHHHHHHHHHHHHH."*

Ronja started playing her crystal bowls to create additional energies for this ceremony. She called in Buddha Ganesh, Merlin, The Lemurian Council of the Cosmic Heart & Light and all of the highest, benevolent Cosmic Light Beings who wanted to support them in their ceremony.

Nina said, "Oh my God, they all are here and I see Sarah in the middle. The Light Beings are surrounding us in a circle and Sarah looks like a blue Avatar. Sarah is telling us her name is Anukah, which means 'The Guided One'. She is saying that she is from a different star system, connected to Sirius. And now, I see all the dragons are coming in."

Kai said, "Yes, my dragon friends are here! They are with me always." He got up and rearranged the formation of his crystal grid and spoke in a deep, rough voice, *"Madakacho edastabaga ochtachtedanoda edachoetaga."*

Yes, Kai had been speaking the dragon language more and more recently since he had been working with the dragon energies during the meditation calls. He was learning how to work with the dragons. They were teaching him different ways to use his magical sword and master his gifts.

As Kai rearranged the grid, Nina saw, in her mind's eye, many dragons flying into the center of the circle. These dragons appeared to be in different sizes and colors. They brought in the energies of New Earth, which were based on unconditional love; the energies of the 5th Dimension. The dragons also told Kai that they were the protectors of New Earth.

In that moment, Nina remembered that during one of the meditation calls, they saw them all entering New Earth over a Rainbow Bridge. They all agreed to step fully forward and embody these New Earth energies. They accepted the unknown and were given the guidance to stay in the NOW, which was the only thing they needed to do. They were guided to send down a cord to the Crystalline Grid of New Earth. They received the information, that a onetime cord connection will always keep them in New Earth.

Nina again was aware of Sarah, still appearing as the blue Avatar, sitting in meditation pose in the middle of the circle. Now, she saw golden sparkles radiating out of Sarah's emerald green heart space.

Ronja saw Dhalia, the Pleiadian priestess, stepping forward, and spoke for her, *"Godaheda manaka. Okahada onameta ga.* We, the Lemurian Council of the Cosmic Heart & Light, are welcoming you."

For the first time, Ronja spoke for Dahlia and translated, *"Godoheda anahata madadoda gedaha!"*

"We have been working with you for quite some time and now, we have instructions for you."

"Obageta godana hestaada godonata bedaga. Edahona Madagoda Ehenamanata ka."

"The dark energies have increased on Earth. But do not fear, as ultimately nothing happens without a soul's agreement."

"Madadoga enaba. Gaschtehada godaneha makadehata edaga!"

"We do know that this is hard for you to comprehend. But the law of the universe is based on love and integrity. Finding God within and evolving to the highest 'God Love frequency' is the plan."

"Maktadoda Enahagate edagoda menedoa bakaorahata getanaka."

"Even the creation of the Matrix was all souls' agreement. Human souls wanted to evolve in the fastest way. The Matrix was allowed because through suffering, one is challenged to evolve quickly. If everyone lived in bliss, harmony and peace all the time, no one would be motivated to change and expand."

"Madadoka egnahada anaheta goronamanina estavatahenagoda edaga."

"We want to gift you with the experience of cosmic, unconditional love to understand better."

The group accepted with gratitude and all the Light Beings started to hum. The Star Team was guided to tone with them. Ezrael, still with his eyes open, saw golden and white light coming in from the Cosmic Light Beings. He became aware that this light created a powerful field around them. His mom, still in the middle of the circle, started to emanate beautiful, white light as well; so much light, that she could hardly be seen anymore. It almost looked like she turned into a beam of light.

As they continued humming together with the Star Beings, they all experienced a feeling of love inside their hearts. They were in awe. There was so much unconditional love and benevolence, which they had never felt before. This bliss state was almost unbearable and brought tears into their eyes.

The group started to hold hands and felt so much gratitude for this gift of sharing this magical experience with each other.

After a long time of humming, Fiandra, the Sirian, stepped forward and spoke, which Nina shared, "Please, do not worship us Higher Dimensional Beings. Humans have it ingrained in their DNA to worship something that is outside of them and superior. We do want you to understand that we are all a part of your consciousness. We are a part of you! You are Starseeds in human bodies and just starting to remember who you are. You have lived on other planets and have participated in the Ascension Process many times before. You are here, old souls, to do it again. Trust that there is nothing for you to learn, rather, it is for you to remember. We are all ONE and only love is real. Have compassion for yourself when you go through dark times, and understand, that in every situation, your soul has agreed to this human experience. Know that everything always happens for your highest good. You must understand this concept to become the Masters and to continue learning in the fastest way possible."

All of them felt very intense energies coming in and a lot of heat in their crown chakras.

For the first time, Ronja was experiencing a sensation of her body dematerializing and being ONE with all existence. She could not help crying out of pure joy and bliss.

All of a sudden, Todd had his first vision. He saw himself as a white wizard working with white dragons and crystal skulls. He was the Master of the skulls. He saw himself placing specific skulls underneath pyramid structures on Planet Earth, knowing they would be found at the right time. He carried the wisdom of how to access the messages and codes of the skulls, as he remembered that he had been the one who programmed them.

Todd could not logically explain what was happening, and somehow, he knew this all to be correct information. He also received the knowing that he had worked with the element of snow to bring in purity, peace and transformation.

Suddenly, Todd spoke Light Language for the first time, "*dididididididiiiddddddddududduduudddddduduudu dididiiidiiiddiiiiddii.*"

All were excited to hear Todd speak.

Nina continued to speak for Fiandra, the Sirian, "We are gifting you with a DNA activation today by transmitting high benevolent frequencies. If the frequencies become too intense for you, please start breathing deeply in and out of the mouth."

They all immediately felt the vibration and started to sway as the energies flowed into the back of their heads, up to their crown chakras, circling back down through their bodies and out of their feet into Mother Earth.

Ezrael could not believe his eyes, as all of a sudden, he saw his mom as the Universe, being the Universe. He felt the vastness of her being and her God-like presence. In the next moment, his mom spoke to him, "Ezrael, what you are experiencing and feeling about me is also in you. Please close your eyes and receive this gift now."

So Ezrael closed his eyes and felt the energies coming into his body and he started to weep. He could not stop crying because he realized that this was one of the key remembering's which he and all souls longed for in this life. In this moment, he also realized it was not about what lives he had before, or what he could do, instead it was about the gift of feeling God within himself.

In the moment when Ezrael finally started to surrender his need to know, he actually started receiving an insight that he was Pleiadian. He experienced the bliss of remembering mixed with extreme sadness for being away from his planet for so long. Ezrael now was aware that he had worked with all of these friends so many times before and he felt grateful to be back with soul family. Now, he understood what it meant when his mom said, "welcome home".

Every one of them had tears flowing down their cheeks, as they sat in the magic of receiving these beautiful, cosmic, unconditional love energies.

In the next moment, Ezrael, eyes still shut, saw Sarah shift back into her blue Avatar form. He was keenly aware now that for the first time his special Sight also worked with his eyes closed.

Sarah looked at Ezrael and said, "My soul has agreed to experience and transmute the dark energies. I am a Master myself and know how to work in the Quantum Field. Do not worry about me, Ezrael. All the work we are doing for ourselves is not only for us. This is an illusion. When we heal something in us, we also heal it for everyone in the Omniverse. It is all quantum and we are part of it all."

Sarah continued to speak to Ezrael, "We carry the energies of the Emerald Circle of the Stars. It is finally safe and it is time to bring these energies back to Earth. We carry the wisdom of the sacred Circle of Oneness from the Stars, and it will be taught again."

After a pause, Sarah suddenly spoke with urgency, "Ezrael bring in the code! Bring in the code!"

Ezrael started to shake and could not stop. While his new friends continued to speak in Light Language, he had another vision. He saw himself in a crystal city, in a pyramid structure, levitating in meditation pose. Someone else was present in the pyramid with him, but he could not see this person clearly. Ezrael saw himself radiating powerful energies out through his heart and eventually, these energies emanated from his entire body. In the next moment, he saw a large Ankh appear in front of him. The Ankh started spinning and he was suddenly within the center of it, looking at a huge infinity symbol above him. Next, Ezrael was moving up towards the center point of the Infinity. As he flew through this center point, he was transported into the Universe and was riding on a red dragon towards a bright planet.

When he landed on this planet, a group of Light Beings escorted him to a large space, which had many golden machines. He saw a small, old humanoid working on these machines. This Being smiled, introduced himself as Imukah, and welcomed him to the Central Sun transmission station.

He gave Ezrael a piece of paper with a code written on it. Ezrael read the numbers: 31, 31, 16, 18, 57, 31.

Imukah explained that this was the code for the new activation portal, which Ezrael had just had created while flying through the infinity symbol. Imukah said activating the code will help him and others to remember their gifts and abilities of other lifetimes. This coded needed to be shared with the group immediately. Ezrael gave thanks, started to fly back on his dragon and in the next moment, he found himself back in Ronja's room with his friends.

Ezrael promptly addressed the group, "I am going to give you an activation code which gives us access to an energetic Quantum portal. See it in a non-linear way. Instead, envision the numbers collapsing into each other, as the code is quantum."

Ezrael repeated the code out loud, "31, 31, 16, 18, 57, 31."

They all envisioned the numbers as instructed and all of a sudden, they saw themselves in a beautiful crystalline city, and knew it was Lemuria. They could hardly believe what was transpiring. There was a feeling of pure high consciousness energies; total unity consciousness, peace and integrity. They experienced a sense of freedom like never before. They were humbled and filled up with emotion as they all remembered these energies.

They all had visions of themselves in Lemuria and received teachings from their higher selves. The group sat in silence for quite some time and suddenly the visions ended and the Light Beings disappeared as well. They knew their work was completed and they closed the ceremony with joyous toning.

Sarah had a grin on her face after she had closed her meditation with gratitude. Her energy field was clear and felt strong again. She decided to go for a walk and offer some tobacco to Mother Gaia and the Ancestors for the blessing they all had just received.

After they closed their session, no one spoke for a while. They were in awe and astounded by what just happened. The Cosmic Light Beings instructed them to keep their experience to themselves for at least a week, to properly integrate the energies individually, before sharing with each other or others.

Kai, Nina, Todd and Ezrael helped Ronja to put her room back in order. They all embraced each other and said goodbye. Ezrael was the last to leave and said to Ronja, surprising himself, "I do need to remember you. Somehow, I feel if I remember you, I will remember myself."

Ronja smiled and replied, "If it is for you to find out, then you will. It is not for me to share. The only thing I know is that I had to find you, and I did. And now, my contract is fulfilled."

Ezrael left Ronja's feeling even more excited about seeing everyone again tomorrow night for the

Full Moon Ceremony at his house. He picked up dinner and was looking forward to seeing how his mom was doing and to share dinner with her. He was grateful to have been shown his mother's multidimensional self. As he walked home, he thought about how wonderful the world would be if everyone on the planet could experience the pure love energies they had just received. He sent this wish out to the Universe, then said "thank you" with confidence, as if his wish had already been granted.

Imero received a telepathic report that the battery charging station had a sudden drop of energy and went down to 50%. Imero was shocked that it went down so quickly. He sensed what had happened and said, "The Lemurians! Those annoying Lemurians! Why can't they just stop bothering me!"

Imero sent telepathic information to the Martian, who quickly responded by increasing the lower frequency transmission from Mars to Earth, to maximum power. Imero had to accept the fact that these fluctuations were inevitable until Occuna's Solar Eclipse Interference was launched. But something needed to happen NOW!

CHAPTER 17

The First Cosmic Language of Light Ceremony

Finally, the Full Moon Ceremony night was here and people were already gathering at Sarah's house. The Star Team had arrived an hour earlier to help Sarah with the set up. Kai was guided to create four grids outside of the fire pit; one in each corner. It was a beautiful summer night and the fire was already burning strong. The guests placed their dishes on the table for the potluck afterwards and settled on blankets around the fire area to wait for the ceremony to start. Sarah held a team meeting with Ezrael, Ronja, Nina, Kai and Todd on how to hold the space and assist her in facilitating the ceremony. Each one received a specific assignment for which direction to cover.

While the Star Team stood around watching Kai finish his last grid, two teenage girls walked towards them. Their names were Valerie and Olivia. Valerie had long, reddish, brown hair and Olivia short, brown hair. Both had brown eyes.

Valerie said, "Hey, what are you up to? These grids are very powerful. I hope you know that they connect to the Crystalline Grid on Earth!"

"Yes, you are correct and I guess you are one of us!" Kai said with a grin and introduced himself to the girls.

Ezrael, Ronja and Nina gathered around the them and said "hello" as well.

Valerie said, "You all seem like you are on a mission."

Nina replied, "Yes, we are. Dark forces have increased on Earth, and we were guided to work with our Guides tonight to bring in more love energy to the planet."

"That sounds perfect," Valerie continued, "We have experienced this too. That is why we came tonight. Maybe we can all work together. I am really good at playing in the Quantum Field. I guess you could call me a a rule buster, more or less. I love to co-create new energies and creative solutions, just because we can and it is time. My good friend Olivia, just started to receive Mayan codes over the last week and is getting instructions from her Higher Self and Guides on how to work with them. We might be of help."

Ezrael said, "Welcome, the more the merrier. We need everyone at the moment."

It was time for ceremony to start. The backyard was filled with people, many carrying drums and rattles. The Star Team, along with their two new friends, stood in a cross formation around the fire. Sarah smudged everyone and then opened the ceremony by saying, "Welcome everyone to our first Cosmic Light Language Ceremony. We have gathered tonight to be of service to the Earth and the Cosmos by celebrating our Divinity. This ceremony will not follow the rules of a regular traditional ceremony and going with the flow is the structure. This is a co-creation, meaning all of your participation is needed to raise the ceremonial energy of healing to its greatest potential."

Sarah continued, "After opening the Ceremony, we are going to tone together. Please bring in your soul essence with your unique tone. This will increase the energies and invoke the Higher, Multidimensional Light Beings to join us. After that we are going to use the right brain, meaning only Light Language will be spoken. It is not about understanding the language, rather, it is the frequency, which will activate your DNA. Do not be surprised if you start speaking the Language of Light for the first time tonight. Stay present and in your heart. Trust when you are guided to speak, I am encouraging you to speak. Do not hold back. Let us all show up 200 percent, and we can make the impossible possible!"

Sarah, called in the four directions, connected everybody to the Crystalline Grid of the Earth, and called in Mother Gaia, Father Sun, Grandmother Moon and Grandfather Sky. Buddha Ganesh was invited to be present, to transmute and amplify the energies and to bring peace. Then Sarah spoke in a commanding voice, *"Madaheda godaneta aka!* Aho!"

Everyone replied by saying, "Aho."

She continued, "We invite in the highest benevolent frequencies of the Pleiadians, Sirians, Arcturians and Orians. Please be with us here tonight! *Odaheda manaheta adodaha aka!* Aho!"

All replied again with, "Aho."

Sarah continued, "We call in the Lemurian Council of the Cosmic Heart & Light! Please be with us here tonight! *Godaheda manadoda Aka!* Aho!"

The group replied again with, "Aho."

Sarah finished the opening by calling in the highest, benevolent forces of the Andromeda Council, the Ascended Masters as well as all Guides, who work with everyone present. Last but not least, she called in the Creator, who resides in all.

All responded with 'Aho' again, they started to tone the sound 'Ahhh'.

The toning invocation got louder and louder and after a while it sounded like a symphony. The energy shifted through the toning and created a magical and powerful quantum space.

Imero, Ammagant, and the members of 'the Gedoha Clan' were alarmed. An emergency meeting was called. All travelled to Inner Earth immediately. Occuna was invited and all were hoping for his powerful presence and guidance. Action needed to be taken NOW.

Ronja started to speak, *"Aktagoda madagoda ektaeta godaheda estodeda agonata gedaha!"* She received a vision of a blind, small man, who introduced himself as Nilrem. He made it clear that he was not Master Merlin, but just, Nilrem, who offered to teach her about the different spaces of the Quantum

Field. She was excited and open to learning more. He guided her through a bluish-golden door and asked her to sit in a chair in a vast dark space. She was made aware that the heart was the major attractor point of the quantum field energies and felt the energies being drawn to her. She came to understand that the more she expanded her own heart space, the stronger the magnetic force became. Ronja intuitively knew to focus on sending love out from her heart to all.

Kai spoke, bringing in the dragon energies, *"Echtideda manineda echtahedo gedaka."*

He held a stick in his hand and started to swirl the stick around, as if it was a wizard's wand. Kai combined the energies he just had created with his crystal grids to generate a vortex of high vibrational energy, which he sent out to the whole world and the Cosmos.

A number of other people were also speaking in the Cosmic Language of Light, and Ezrael started to shake. He felt as if dark energies entered him, but wondered how this could be possible, since it was a high vibrational ceremony. He looked around and saw two people who had a lot of dark energies around them. He saw the energies emanating out to others in the ceremony.

Suddenly, he saw this big, white elephant coming into the ceremony space. He watched as he transmuted all the dark energies with a blink of an eye and a smile. He felt better instantly.

Suddenly, Daliah, the Pleiadian Priestess, stood in front of Ezrael. She looked into his eyes with a friendly smile and said, "I am here to help you remember. Although your cosmic name is Lazumar, in Lemuria you were called Yahee."

Daliah snapped her fingers right in front of Ezrael's face and instantly, he was teletransported to Lemuria. He saw himself in a temple, sitting on a chair and there was a line of people waiting to see him. He started to remember that in this incarnation, he was a Master and a High Priest. He gave blessings and offered consultations to people while the woman beside him, Yaheema, was there holding healing ceremonies. Yaheema worked with flowers and plants creating remedies from their essences. He remembered them working together like this for hundreds of years. He knew that their life span in Lemuria was much longer, due to their fully activated DNA. He noticed they both had dark brown skin color and black hair. Yaheema's hair was very long and shiny. To his surprise, she had green eyes, though his were brown, as was usual with most Lemurians.

Suddenly, Yaheema looked at him with a smile and showed him the red and green dragons, drawn on each of the palms of her hands. Ezrael, knew this was a message. Yet, he could not understand what these dragons on her palms meant.

All of a sudden, the scene changed and he saw himself working in a pyramid with codes and drawings. Ezrael saw himself with this woman again holding ceremony in the pyramid. They were sitting around a small fire meditating. Then they looked at each other and exchanged energies. Next, the woman put a magic potion into the fire and to his surprise, he started to levitate a few feet off the ground. He was still sitting in meditation pose.

Suddenly, he was back at the ceremony with Dhalia, who was still smiling at him.

As the Ceremony continued, Todd saw himself as a white wizard again. He called in the white dragons and unicorns. He played with his imagination, intending to bring in as much light as possible to the ceremony. In the Cosmos he was called Gorunda, the White Wizard. He was excited about how well it was working and started to believe in his powers. In his mind's eye, he saw 13 crystal skulls around the ceremony circle. Todd knew that this was a message for him to start working with crystal skulls in this life.

Nina also had visions during the ceremony about being in Lemuria. She saw herself working with Sarah and they both were historians in this Lemurian timeline. Nina was the story collector. In this lifetime, Nina loved to visit the different galactic civilizations, to collect and bring back their ancient, sacred stories to the Lemurian library. Nina saw that they were using a crystalline tablet technology to store all the information.

Valerie saw Ganesh, who was a blue elephant, laughing, as he danced around her. She always asked for guidance and never received any in all these years. This was a big mystery for her, and she could not fully grasp the reason, yet. A big piece of the puzzle was still missing. Valerie knew everything was in Divine Order. Patience was needed. She found out that her cosmic name was Maheta.

Valerie knew she was here to break the rules and that the impossible was always possible. She was also committed to the highest good of all. She envisioned marshmallow sprinkles coming into the space, tribbles and secret sauce, which she believed always shifts everything to the better. Little did she know what impact her imagination had in the Quantum Field.

Valerie was connected quantumly all the time. She received that gift a long time ago because her heart was so pure and her mission to shift mass consciousness was sacred. She was not fully aware of who she was in the multidimensional, cosmic realms, yet. She always saw herself visiting a spaceship that had a large dome and an amphitheater, where beings from all over the Cosmos gathered for important meetings. Her wish was that one day soon, her ship would be traveling around Earth and holding activation seminars and celebrations for the newly awakened humans. She believed whatever you can imagine, is absolutely possible.

The energies of the ceremony continued to increase in a magical way. The participants were joyously following Sarah's lead in toning and chanting. The beat of the drums and the sound of the rattles, combined with the human voices, resonated like a symphony throughout the neighborhood and beyond into the quantum, multidimensional fields.

Olivia received specific codes, which were being activated during ceremony. She had a vision of herself in a life back in the time of the Mayans. Annaya Maya was her Mayan name. She was part of a team who calculated and created the calendars, many of which are still being used by some today. Olivia was aware that the messages and guidance, which she had received during this Mayan life, came from the Stars.

Next, she saw golden books appear right in front of her eyes. Olivia witnessed the energies of the wisdom, drawings and symbols from these sacred books getting activated within her being. She felt this energy very strongly. Her upper body started to sway. Suddenly, Olivia received the insight that she had many prior life times as a Shaman.

Sarah worked with her Cosmic Guides, Dhalia and Fiandra, during the Ceremony. They worked together to open the two time capsules to increase compassion on Earth. Sarah knew that it could only happen when the energies of this ceremony were aligned with the energies of the Earth and the Cosmos. She knew it was almost time.

Suddenly, Sarah felt so much energy flowing through her body, more than she had ever experienced before. It was so intense, that she knew the only way to handle these energies was to totally surrender to the higher, benevolent forces. Sarah picked up her activator crystal, which was a large, multicolored Andara crystal. This crystal carried Lemurian energies and came to her recently. Her body started to sway, while she spoke the Language of Light in a loud, strong voice, *"Enanahea aka. Madageda Ohado Bastagada! Netadorda Gohabaheda Anaheta Godaha!"*

While Sarah spoke, she traced symbols in the air with her crystal. She started to shake, her voice became louder as she held the activator crystal up in the air over the fire. Suddenly, she saw the two time capsules opening. She relaxed and laughed wholeheartedly, filled with joy because she had completed her mission.

As dark forces gathered in the Inner Earth meeting room, they received a report that the battery charging station went down to 35%. The situation was becoming even more urgent and all were in agreement that drastic measures were called for NOW!

Imero felt himself getting weaker and weaker. He was just glad that he even had the strength to make it to the meeting. Ammagant felt weak as well. They both were perplexed and angry. Imero had informed Ammagant about his unfortunate downgrade in position. Imero cringed just thinking about the loss of his Emperorship, and now serving as Occuna's disciple.

Now, Ammagant was concerned about losing his position and was hoping to have time to talk to Occuna during the meeting, if Occuna showed. Ammagant was ready to do whatever was needed to be allowed to stay on Earth. It just did not seem fair. He had done so much good work for Imero and the dark forces. Ammagant felt he deserved a second chance.

Shortly after the time capsules opened, Sarah closed the ceremony with an extended toning period. She gave thanks to all the participants, all the Light Beings and to the directions. She encouraged everyone to stay for the potluck dinner to give everyone a chance to ground and to connect. Sarah explained that some may experience minor symptoms from the DNA activation because the body might need to release for a few days. Sarah shared that it was important to release and to surrender and to drink a lot of water.

Everyone stayed and enjoyed the potluck dinner afterwards. The air was filled with magic and joy, and it felt like a celebration. The Star Team gathered together for a few minutes and shared whatever they felt guided to share. They all knew that the ceremony was a great success and that it was also a preparation for what was to come.

Valerie and Olivia exchanged contacts with the others and were invited to the daily meditation calls and to the next gathering for the solar eclipse. They were both very excited about finding their soul tribe.

Ronja and Valerie had so much fun hanging out after the ceremony and then walked home together, talking and laughing the whole way. Both knew they were going to be great friends. They had such a deep, easy connection from the start, as if they knew each other forever.

Todd, Kai, Olivia and Nina stayed late into the night, talking around the fire. Ezrael hung out with his friends for a short time, and then needed to be by himself. By the end of the evening, he realized he was becoming overwhelmed by the chatter of all the people and decided to retreat to his favorite meditation spot in the woods.

Ezrael could not stop thinking about his vision in the temple. He wondered who this woman was. He wished that he could understand her message of her showing her palms with the red and green dragons. Somehow, he knew, that if he resolved this piece of the puzzle, he would find peace.

CHAPTER 18

The Counteract

The Beings, attending the Inner Earth meeting, sat in silence and tension was felt by all. Everyone was hoping that Occuna would show his presence during the meeting, but he had not appeared yet. Kamit, the Reptilian, Ledura, the Malbecian, Hedoha, the Insectoid, and Kedrek, the Martian, were already present with Imero and Ammagant.

Imero started to address the group in an angry voice, "I told you that we should not underestimate the Lemurians! They are defeating us again."

Kamit stopped him right away with a stern voice and said, "Imero, we are not starting the meeting like this. Thank you for coming and let me open the discussion, as I am the leader of this meeting and of 'the Gedoha Clan'. You are out of line to interrupt me and bring in chaotic energies. This will not help us to move forward. Imero, do you understand!"

Imero apologized and became quiet. He knew that he needed all of them to help him get his power back on Earth and to keep his newly downgraded disciple position under Occuna. Yes, Imero was worried for the first time ever that he might need to leave the planet forever. So Imero surrendered his ego for a short period and listened.

Kamit continued, "Imero, give us a status report on how Occuna's Interference Transmission is progressing!"

Imero, who had calmed down now, replied, "It is still working just fine. The transmission was sent down to Earth and it has affected many people so far. The battery charging station has been showing some fluctuation. For a while after the transmission, we had an increase to 90%, which was exciting to experience. Unfortunately, the Lemurians have started to gather and we have seen a decrease in power recently.

I do not understand. It is just a small amount of people. Nevertheless, they seem to have more power than all the rest of the humans who are under mind control."

Imero continued, "We had a connection to these annoying monsters through a human boy, but somehow, he escaped out of the Matrix and now is untraceable. The problem is, when humans disconnect from the Matrix, they are invisible to us and can work under the radar. When they gather, the battery charging station loses strength. That is what we have observed. It is now down to a new low of 35%, which has never happened before."

All the meeting attendees gasped at this news and started to whisper to each other.

Imero, in a loud voice, to be heard over the group, said, "There is some good news!"

Imero waited for all to be quiet and continued, "Occuna gave me another device, which will be a devastating transmission for Earth during the Solar Eclipse. I have the new device in my possession and I am ready to activate it at the exact moment of the Solar Eclipse. It will capitalize on the moment of darkness. I expect this will work to perfection and we will be back to full power."

Kamit thanked Imero for his report and asked Kedrek, the Martian, "What is the update on the dark energy transmission?"

Kedrek, replied, "I am sad to report that our transmission from Mars is not working anymore. Somehow a Rainbow Bridge was created around the Earth, and it filters out any bad behavior it seems. I am not sure if the Guardians are going to be involved. But I guarantee you, if the Guardians become aware of our little plot, we will be done for good."

Kamit said with concern, "Yes, this is all very concerning. We can only do our best. We must not stop our work due to fear of being detected by the Guardians. As you all know, the Guardians only interfere in the worst-case scenarios, and our intentions for Earth are not that bad yet. We are not talking about blowing up the planet or anything."

They all chuckled a little and Kamit continued, "So let us trust that it all will be fine and we will not get detected. However, time is of the essence, as we do not have much time left before the frequency of Earth becomes too high for us to survive. Our Reptilian civilization is struggling. Most of our people have already surrendered to the light and love energies and are already cooperating and going through the rehabilitation process. As I see it, if we fail, we only have a couple of options. We can also surrender, rehabilitate and stay on the planet or we need to leave before we perish. As you know, the Queen and the King will never surrender. They will fight until the bitter end. Many of us have already been taken off the planet. The Andromeda Council has been offering to relocate us to a new habitat. This is all very dreadful. We never thought it would come that far after all these thousands of years."

Everyone was quiet and in a state of shock, hearing for the first time, how bad the situation really was.

Hedoha, the Insectoid, gave her report next, "I am sorry to announce, I have more bad news as well. The small group of people, who were loyal to the cause, left me. They are enjoying the new energies of love in Inner Earth. Not sure what these Lemurians have done, but somehow, they managed to send 'the emerald green love energies' directly into Inner Earth. They have never been happier. I am the last one left from my clan who is still for the dark."

Kedrek, the Martian, responded, "Enough with the energies of defeat! We are not done, yet. Just because the battery charging station is down to 35%, does not mean we are defeated."

Imero continued, "Thanks to the start of Occuna's transmission last week, the Earth is getting bombarded with lower vibrational frequencies. I believe it is because of this interference, we still have 35% battery life left. Otherwise, it would be down to zero. I am surprised Occuna has not joined us. Tonight, is a pivotal moment for us. On Earth this Full Moon has really hurt us. As you know, the humans have celebrated this night monthly for ages, following the lineage of their ancestors. These Lemurians, who remember their ancient ceremonies, are just destroying everything we have planned. "

Kedrek, the Martian continued, "It seems like we need to work on our defense strategy. We need to create a grid work, which will prevent these ugly *'love energies'* from spreading. How can we do this? I wonder?"

In the next moment, a cold wind blew into the meeting room, and they knew where it was coming from. Occuna appeared, and everyone was excited and thankful for his appearance.

Occuna started to speak, as if he heard the whole prior meeting conversation, "Yes, we do not have any time to waste. Having a defense strategy for the years to come is a very good idea. The new Rainbow Bridge is hurting us. My concern is that the Guardians will love this new invention of Imukah so much, that it will be reproduced in the Galaxies, which could seriously hurt my authority."

Occuna continued, "Imukah and The Lemurian Council of the Cosmic Heart & Light are responsible for this creation. Our mission was not as undetected as we had hoped. Right now, we need to stay low and work on our defense strategy as much as possible, so we can complete our final attack during the Solar Eclipse, which fortunately, is approaching very fast."

With a smile on his face, Occuna announced, "I need everyone to know that I have taken over Earth now and Imero has accepted the position to be my disciple."

All of them were shocked about this news. It immediately prompted them to worry about the safety of their own positions. They knew that Occuna could do anything he wanted to do.

Occuna continued, "I am willing to give Imero another chance with my new Interference invention, which will be activated during the Solar Eclipse. If he does not perform well, he will be teletransported to another planet. Be aware, that all of this can happen to you as well. Your Gedoha Clan has lost power. For now, it is important that you listen to me, so we can get our strength and power back on Earth."

Kamit replied, "I do understand Occuna, and I think you stepping in as our leader, is very helpful at the moment. Imero and Ammagant are quite affected from the low power of the battery charging station, and I have to admit, it affects me, the King and the Queen as well. So thank you, Occuna. Let us finish this meeting quickly, as we know that dark energies grouped together can be detected. We have no time to waste."

Ledura, the Malbecian, continued, "We had a defense system in place for Malbec, which, as you know. Unfortunately, it did not work and we destroyed ourselves because of a failure in this system. The good news is, the ones who have survived, have continued to work on this system. Actually, it is working well right now. We could use it here on Earth."

Kamit asked, "Can you assure us that it won't blow up Earth as well? How can we trust that this intervention will not cause our own demise?"

Occuna interjected, "I have overseen the construction of this new defense system and I know it is working to perfection."

Kamit said, "I guess you have your hands in every fire."

Occuna replied proudly, "That is why I am the Dark Emperor of the Galaxies. I know how the Quantum Field works. I am not going to even go into the powerful DNA configurations, which I have developed myself. I am a Master of the Universal Quantum Field!"

All were in awe and envious of Occuna's powerful dark gifts.

Occuna demanded, "Ledura, you will activate the defense system right before the Solar Eclipse starts. The only thing you will need to do at that time is to put these codes into your defense system controller: 5, 4, 5, 4, 5, 9, 9. Do you understand? This is how we will connect your powerful defense system with my interference grid on Earth. It will bypass the Rainbow Bridge during my blast off event, at the time of darkness during the Solar Eclipse. I assure you, it will work beautifully. And, it cannot be detected by anyone in the Galaxies!" With these words Occuna started to laugh, enjoying his own magnificence.

Kamit was very hopeful, and said, "All your solutions sound wonderful. It seems like we have a powerful strategy in place. Before we close and get back to work, we need to address the situation with Hedoha."

All eyes shifted to Hedoha, the ant like Insectoid, and Kamit continued, "Hedoha, we thank you for standing with us. Right now, we will not be able to support you in overthrowing the Leaders in your civilization. We will revisit this after the Solar Eclipse, when everything is back to normal. You will be a great help to us by continuing to spy, and report to us on the collaborations of your people with the humans against the dark. For now, we all need to work together to assure the success of Occuna's Counteract plan. Does everyone agree?"

All agreed and quickly left the meeting. All were a little paranoid about possible detection by the Intergalactic Peace Federation and the Guardians. Occuna stopped Imero and Ammagant from leaving and said, "Imero and Ammagant, I need to have a word with you before you leave!"

They all sat back down at the table and Occuna said, "I am quite upset about what is happening on Earth. One of you will need to take full responsibility for what is happening here at the moment. It shows me that both of you are incapable of managing Earth. I am not sure what to do about it. I may have to replace you both."

Occuna continued, "As I announced earlier, I am taking over Earth now, to assure a positive outcome of this situation. You must understand that I can be in several places at once and I overhear every conversation in the Galaxies simultaneously. Let us say, almost all of them. There are only a few of the intergalactic meetings to which I do not have access. They carry specific secret frequency codes, which I have not been able to crack yet. But this is not of my concern."

Occuna pounded his fist on the table. Imero and Ammagant jumped.

Occuna stared into their eyes and spoke in a serious tone, "I seem to be doing all the work here. You,

Imero need to come up with a new reconstruction plan for your Matrix, or a new invention pretty soon. I know you are capable of great things, as you have proved me right two thousand years ago. You and Ammagant make a good team. Although I love separation and isolation energies, I know that you need to work together for now, to get something new going. So, get started! I am expecting that your new invention will be powerful. Blow me away! This is going to be your last chance to stay on Earth!"

He got up to leave and then stopped to give one more warning. Occuna looked at Imero and said after a pause, "...Imero, do not mess up the Solar Eclipse transmission!"

With these words, Occuna disappeared.

Imero and Ammagant went back to their home, feeling small and devastated. They were not sure how they would be able to come up with an invention, powerful enough to stop these 'love energies' from spreading at such a rapid pace. It was in times like these, that they wondered whether there was actually a benefit to praying to God. Right now, they knew they needed a miracle to get their powers back.

CHAPTER 19

The Guardians

Occuna spoke the truth, when he shared in the meeting, that there were Intergalactic meetings to which he could not gain access. These were the meetings of the Guardians.

The Guardians were pure consciousness, meaning they were only energy. This consciousness group only appeared in physical matter when their services were needed in the Galaxies. The only time they appeared in physical form was when an intervention was needed in the Omniverse. When they showed themselves in physical matter, they lived on a spaceship. Their ship was larger than any mothership and had a huge dome covering the top. They would appear wherever it was needed, in whatever timeline. The Guardian's ship was fueled by quantum energy and pure God-Consciousness, which was cosmic, unconditional love. The interesting part of its physical manifestation was that the frequencies of the ship totally aligned and mimicked the mathematical frequencies of the Omniverse. The Guardian's ship could shift instantly into different timelines and realities. It could never be accessed or detected from outside sources.

It was time, the Guardians called a meeting and the spaceship appeared in a Galaxy far, far away from Earth. In a Galaxy which was not even detected by humans yet.

It was the Norvardian Galaxy, an amazing galaxy comprising hundreds of beautiful stars and many civilizations. One of them was the Harphoy civilization. They were 8 feet tall, blue Avatar Beings, who were on the same timeline for Ascension as the Earth. They were seeded and being helped by the Sirians as they were going through their Ascension Process. Similar to the way the Pleiadians helped with the Earth's Ascension.

Still, with all the planets on the similar Ascension timeline at the moment, the Earth had an advantage, due to the Lemurian DNA strands. These DNA strands were quantum based and therefore expedited human awakening. It was an invention and gift from the Pleiadians. This was something none of the other civilizations had, and therefore, the planet Earth's Ascension was followed with excitement by all in the Omniverse. The humans were doing what all thought was impossible. The way the humans woke up, united and realized their divinity and the power of unconditional love was unheard of, given the extreme control the dark forces had for so long.

All watching in the Omniverse came to understand that the brilliant creation of Lemuria, by the Pleiadians, was one of the most beautiful and powerful inventions in the Omniverse. And now, as the Lemurian DNA strands were being reactivated in the humans, the energy shifts on Earth were powerfully impacting all the other planets in the Galaxies. Love and gratitude was felt by all in the Omniverse.

Civilizations of all the Galaxies were interested in the Lemurian/Pleiadian DNA structure and many sent farming teams to steal this unique DNA. Due to the protection of the Guardians, the DNA farming was stopped. What these farmers missed was that this DNA worked only together with the energies of Mother Gaia. These DNA strands were useless without the alchemical combination of Gaia's magnetic field, crystalline structures and the activation of the Lemurian humans, who held the secret codes and keys.

The Guardians chose the Norvadian Galaxy for their meeting because the Harphoy's planet, called Vedura, was the polar planet of Earth in the Omniverse. By holding the meeting in this location, they were activating the balancing points of the omniversal grid between these two planets.

The Guardians teletransported hundreds of thousands of the leaders, from only the highest frequency civilizations of the Omniverse, to attend this meeting. Only one member of each civilization was selected to attend. The chosen ones received a telepathic message a split second before the teleportation happened. Everyone knew that being called to a meeting with the Guardians was an honor, as only the purest souls who had achieved their highest evolution, were able to attend.

The Guardians balanced and aligned their own frequency as well as the frequencies of all who attended the meeting. This assured that all would be resonating on an equal energy plane. This process was pure alchemy and no easy task. In order to come into physical form, the Guardians needed to reduce their frequency through the alchemical processes of transduction and transmutation. The frequencies of all attendees needed to be increased to a very high vibration and individually monitored. In this way they were able to maintain the equilibrium of the physical form of each being on the Guardian's ship.

Novix and Merlin sat around a huge fire. Merlin had his wizard stick in his hand and created infinity symbols over the fire, exactly as Sarah did during the Full Moon Ceremony. He was enjoying the energies and was so excited about the potentials for Earth.

Merlin was involved in many other Ascension processes happening simultaneously with other Planets as well. His main responsibility was to be a Guide between the 3rd and the 4th dimensions on Earth, and he loved his work. Yes, there was one Guide for each dimensional bridge, one for every human. He oversaw hundreds of thousands of humans at the same time.

Merlin had several incarnations as a human on Earth, so he intimately understood the human condition, and had the utmost compassion for the human experience. Other Guides, especially on the higher dimensions, did not have this extremely valuable experience.

Master Merlin looked at Novix as he suddenly felt intense energies coming over him, and announced to Novix with a smile, "The Guardians! The Guardians are calling me to a meeting!"

In the next split second, Master Merlin became a beam of light and disappeared right in front of Novix's eyes.

The expansive meeting room on the Guardian's ship quickly filled with all different species of beings. When the flashes of teleported beings stopped, the room was silent and all waited with excited anticipation for the meeting to start.

Suddenly, three Guardians appeared in physical form. Today they chose the body forms of a Sirian, a Pleiadian and a Harphoy.

The meeting was conducted primarily through telepathic communication. They also employed sound vibrations for the integration of major downloads. These downloads were blessings for all attendees to propel the evolution of their civilizations further. The Guardians knew that sound, vibration and light were integral to receiving transmissions.

The Sirian Guardian stepped to the podium and spoke very slowly, *"Mogoohhdoooohaaastaaagoooo-hoooopaaaakaaaadaaaaa. Odhaaaaaaaaaaaaaaheeeeeeeeeeeeegodonamahedaaaaaaaaaaaaaaa."*

His frequency was so high and so quantumly linked that all members received a download from his speech. They received, through this transmission, the vision of unity consciousness and love. It strengthened their knowing of the truth, that the Omniverse was interconnected and all parts of the Galaxies came together as ONE.

It seemed today's meeting was all about the forward movement of the planets in the Ascension Process.

The Sirian Guardian continued to speak, *"Mooooooooooooooooonoooooooaheeeeeeeedaaaaaaa Goooooooooo-hooooooobaaaaaaaaaaaheeeeeedaaaNaaaaaaaamaaaaaaaaanooooooooohaaaaaaaaaadooooooooo-naaaaaaaaaaamooooooooonaaaaaaaaaaaaadeeeeeeegooooooooooooohaaaaaaaaaabaaaaaaaaadeeeeeeeeeeee-nooooooooohaaaaaaaaaadaaaaaaaaaaaaaaabeeeeee."*

While the Guardian was speaking, all attendees received the telepathic information about the 16 ascending planets. The Guardian informed them of how the energy of multiple planets simultaneously ascending, created an instability in the Omniverse, which was foreseen. They showed that these ascending civilizations were suffering, as higher light frequencies beamed through their planetary grids, affecting all life forms. It showed release of lower energies for these civilizations to carry higher light forms. It also showed the resistance of the dark to surrender to love and light.

All the attendees were flashed with a remembrance of feeling what they experienced during their own Ascension. For many, it had been eons and they had forgotten the struggle and how difficult it was, as they now lived in harmony, peace, integrity and bliss. This remembering created compassion in each of the hundreds of thousands of meeting members, which was needed for rebalancing the energies of the Omniverse, healing the instability caused by multiple planets ascending.

The Harphoy Guardian stepped forward and shared, *"Moooooooonoooooooohaaaaaaaaaaheeeeeeetaaaaaaaaaagooooooooooooooooodooooooooooooooraaaaaaaaaasaaaaaaaaaaaabeeeeeeeheeeeeeeeeeetaaaaaaaaaaaaaaaaaaaaaaaaaaaagoooooooooooooooooonooooooooooooooomaaaaaaaaaaaaaaaaaaaaaaaaaaaheeeeeeeeeeeeeeeeeeenaaaaaaaaaaaaaaaaaaaaaaaaaaaaaaaaaaaaaaaaaaaaagoaaaaaaaaaaaaabaaaaaaaaaaaaaaaaaaaa."*

He explained that the Guardians were true, pure God Source and had chosen, due to the instability in the Omniverse, to have one Guardian embodiment in physical form on each ascending planet. The work of this Guardian in physical form on each planet was not to be underestimated.

The Sirian Guardian conveyed the message that the physical manifestation of the Guardian on each planet was "the boots on the ground" in physical form to request intervention for all beings on their planets at all times. The rest of the civilizations did not have the knowledge and power to do so. The Sirian Guardian also wanted to make sure that everyone of the attendees understood that their intervention was hardly necessary due to the work of the Guardians on each planet, who worked purely with compassion, which automatically transmuted dark energies.

The Sirian Guardian asked every attendee to keep their planet on the highest frequency as possible during this crucial time of the Ascension. The Guardian made everyone aware that at this time, their assistance might be called for, if the Omniverse does not stabilize itself with the help of all planets quickly.

Of course, all attendees agreed as they were in the beautiful state of compassion and were aware they would benefit just as much. All knew that the successful ascension completion of all these planets would cause a major expansion and upgrade for all planets in the Omniverse.

Next, the Pleiadian Guardian stepped forward to address the attendees, *"Machtodehadoga, Ehastoradaminada, Ahadeaheta, Nabade Godanehea, Gododoododdoodooddodoodadooodododod……* We, the Guardians, are gifting you with this blessing of Grace to take home to your people to help them stay in the highest frequencies of love and compassion."

The hundreds of thousands of beings felt a split second of energy entering their third eye and their hearts.

The Pleiadian continued, "This is all for now. We thank everyone for joining."

Suddenly, the Guardians disappeared and all attendees were teleported back to their planet.

The Guardians knew to keep these meetings short. Too much time in this higher frequency state, which was required, could be very hard on the attendee's body systems.

What no one knew yet, was that the Guardian representative on Earth was one of the Star Team members. The deep block to this Earth Guardian representative's remembering process was very difficult for her. She lived her life in service for the higher good of all on the planet, with the intention not to leave anyone behind. She was consciously very evolved but could not remember anything about her own multidimensional history, nor did she speak the Language of Light. She was not aware that this was a necessary part of the Divine Plan.

This team member was constantly looking for clarity, and unlike the rest of the group, never received the answers from other light being forms. She just had to trust her own intuition and knowing.

This person was not aware that she did major work on the Guardian's ship every night and that was the reason why she could not remember her dreams. Every day she shifted the planet by transmuting the mass consciousness into a higher vibration. She was not aware of her own powers and what she did for the planet.

This Guardian representative was Valerie, who had no idea about her sacred mission, nor that she embodied the Guardian's energy on Earth. Her deep work in this lifetime was to transmute reptilian DNA, which she chose to carry in her own DNA, and she was on track with the transmutation process. Valerie was aware of her reptilian bloodline, which she took on in a much earlier incarnation as a Reptilian Queen. So far Valerie had not shared this information with anyone. The reptilian Queen of Inner Earth, Kafura, at this moment, was aware of the work Valerie chose to do and was ready to intervene as soon as it was needed. Queen Kafura had no intention of ever surrendering to love and light and she did not even entertain the idea of leaving the planet. Although many of her people were leaving, she knew that when she finally defeated the light, she would be able to reproduce her civilization at a fast speed. The Queen was aware of the dark force's plan and she was ready to support their mission during the Solar Eclipse.

The Guardians worked on a very high level and only intervened when it was necessary, as free choice was honored everywhere in the Galaxies. The Guardians understood the benevolence of God's creation. All is always in alignment with the highest good and expansion of consciousness.

The destruction of Malbec, for example, was not a mistake and was foreseen. There was a benevolent plan behind it that most were not aware of. Nothing in the Universe happens without each soul's agreement, as all are connected in Oneness.

The wars the Malbecians had created were not helping their Ascension Process anymore, and the planet itself struggled to evolve enough to hold a high enough frequency to support the Ascension for its civilization. The Guardians saw the potential to create a parallel world for the Malbecians and also saw the benefits of having an Asteroid belt. The Malbecian leader asked the Guardians for help. Because the Malbecian souls were in total agreement with the Guardians, the malfunction of the planet's war infiltration system, which caused the huge explosion of the planet, was actually a blessing. The Malbecians were teletransported, before the explosion, by the Guardians to a new parallel world. The Malbecians are now already in their 6th Dimension and have succeeded in love and light. The Asteroid belt has helped to protect the higher frequencies on Earth.

The Divine Intelligence is and will always be the big Mystery. All souls are always connected to it, knowingly or unknowingly. The civilizations on Earth and all other ascending planets were born during a time of low frequency, which caused amnesia and a feeling of separation from Source. These ascending civilizations spent their lives working on overcoming this amnesia to rise up to the 5th dimension of unity consciousness and love.

The Guardians protected the law of this Divine Intelligence, which could be found in every particle of the universe and also in each cell of every living being. "As within, as without" and "as above, so below" are simple terms of reflecting this big mystery of life. To find the God Source, Oneness, Divine Love and the powers within, is the divine sacred game. The evolution of consciousness in the Omniverse is sacredly guarded by the Guardians.

The Guardians were always in support of every being in all Galaxies. They operated with the highest integrity in all matters.

No one knew that the Guardians were working directly with Imukah and that a new 5D Matrix was already in creation. This new crystalline Matrix would help connect the humans on Planet Earth to the Divine Intelligence, to feel their Divine essence and to access self-love, integrity and compassion faster. If it worked, this would be a key accelerator in the Earth's Ascension and would be duplicated on all the other ascending planets.

Instructions were given to Tartan, the Mountain Being, who already started working with Ronja and other chosen human beings on Earth, who were creating the 5D Matrix on the earthly plane. All was on track. As it was discussed earlier, the Lemurians, due to their advanced DNA and the power of their unity consciousness, brought something special to the Earth's Ascension that was never ever seen anywhere else in the Omniverse.

This new Crystalline 5D Matrix, supported by the magnetic field of the Earth, would also support the grounding of the 'love energies' and make it possible for humans to stay in high vibrations and bliss during the solar flares. These high frequency solar flares, sent from the Central Sun via the Earth's Sun to the planet, were a planned transmission to accelerate the Ascension process. Everything has been divinely arranged with benevolence.

This new Matrix creation, as well as the Rainbow Bridge, were designed to filter these high frequencies of the solar flares. They were created to help all of humanity to raise their consciousness as fast as possible. Therefore, these high frequencies would be integrated with ease, grace and bliss.

The main purpose of this new Matrix was to strengthen the connection to the Divine Intelligence, which would help all humans to quickly gain access to the pool of creation.

The Guardians and all in the Omniverse were looking forward to seeing the humans getting free from the Matrix of fear. A time when the humans would be able to start creating a better world for themselves, with their own benevolent imagination and enchantment. This magic would be fueled by their remembering of unconditional, Divine Love.

CHAPTER 20

The Final Countdown

The day of the Solar Eclipse was finally here. The hometown of the Lemurian Star Team was filled with tourists. Their town was in the path of totality for the total solar eclipse. The total solar eclipse would happen at 3:33 pm. The Star Team had agreed to meet at Sarah's house to hold a private Fire Ceremony in her backyard during this time. All were excited and could not wait to gather at 3 pm. They were not aware that an urgency was felt by all Light Workers around the planet. Many different groups around the world were also preparing to hold ceremonies or meditations during the time of the Eclipse.

Although billions of people were living on Earth, only a small percentage of Light Workers were needed to unite and use their powers to shift the energies of the entire collective to more light. Just 0.5% of the population was needed to ensure and accelerate the Ascension process of the Earth and humanity. This small group of people were beautifully connected to the Crystalline Grid. This made them keenly aware of their powers to shift consciousness by pure intent. The intention of connecting to the Divine Intelligence within themselves and the grid was all that was needed to do so. These Light Workers, like the Star Team, carried the activated Lemurian DNA.

Ezrael and Sarah were preparing the fire for the ceremony and this time, not much needed to be done. Sarah had set up a loudspeaker outside in the yard, and both were listening to one of Sarah's favorite songs from Peter Kater and Snatam Kaur, "The Heart of the Universe". This was a song which always made Sarah feel connected to the Earth and the Cosmos. As she sang Light Language along to the song, she felt "the Oneness with all there is". Ezrael enjoyed listening to his mom while cleaning out the fire pit.

As Ezrael strategically stacked the wood in the fire pit, he asked Sarah, "Mom, I was wondering if you are aware of your dragon and what color it is?"

Sarah looked at him with surprise, smiled and said, "This is an interesting question for you to ask me. Yes, I do. The name of my dragon is Ladorra, and her color is purple. What makes you ask?"

Ezrael, who was still curious to find the answer to the mystery of the two dragons on the woman's hands in his vision, replied, "I had a vision of a life I had back in Lemuria and there was a woman in it, who was so familiar to me. We held ceremonies together and served the planet for hundreds of years. I was a priest and she was a priestess. We meditated together and somehow, I knew that when we unite our forces, I could do the impossible. I even seemed to overcome gravity by using pure consciousness thought forms. I believe this woman gave me a message during the vision. She showed me her palms. One palm had a red dragon drawn on it, and on the other palm, a green one. Then she brought the dragons together by bringing her hands, palms facing me, up to her heart space. That was it. I do not know more. I remember I once had a vision of myself and other people riding dragons, but I do not recall my dragon's color, nor any of the others. Honestly, I do not even remember who the other people were."

Ezrael became silent and continued to enjoy building the fire.

Sarah looked at him and replied, "Trust that you will know the meaning of the message and remember more at the right time. There is no need to push it. When you surrender and have patience, it can come to you faster, with ease and grace."

Ezrael replied with a deep sigh, "But Mom, I know there is something I have to remember now. There is an urgency about it. I cannot tell you more. I just know I need to remember now!" Ezrael was frustrated.

Sarah received an intuitive hit, looked at Ezrael and said, "Do you remember the song, which I sent you long time ago, and asked you to download for meditations?"

Ezrael could not remember and asked, "Which one, Mom?"

Sarah answered, "The song 'Adiemus' by Karl Jenkins, from the album 'Songs of Sanctuary'. This is the sacred song that helped me start to remember. I listened to only this song, over and over, during many meditations. I received clarity and many insights about past lives and my purpose, while listening to it. I have a feeling it might help you on your journey as well. Maybe if you go inside and meditate with this song, you will gain some clarity. Call in your Higher Self, or better yet, call in all of your multidimensional Higher Selves."

Ezrael was excited and said, "Yes, Mom, I will do this right now. Thank you for your guidance." Ezrael went over to his mom, gave her a big hug and said, "I love you so much, Mom! Thank you for always guiding me. I do not know what my life would be like without you. I will definitely miss you when I go on my vacation with dad and Carina tomorrow."

"I will miss you too, my love. But as you know, I will be traveling myself. When we come back, we will share about our adventures," Sarah said with a smile. "Now go! Do your inner work. Nothing is outside of you. That is the big illusion. All is within you!"

Ezrael thanked her again and went into the house. He already knew how to create sacred space for himself. First, Ezrael put his cell phone on airplane mode, found the song and set it to play on auto repeat. He lit a candle, burned incense, smudged himself with white sage, and sat down in meditation pose on the floor in his bedroom.

Sarah was guided to start the fire a little early. She played the song "Directions" by Nahko and Medicine for the People. Soon, she found herself singing along in Light Language. She opened the space for Ezrael and called in all the forces and directions to help her son on his path of finding his Divinity and the knowing that he was always connected to all there is. Next, she said to the fire, as if she was speaking to Ezrael, "You need to look at this Ezrael! It is time that you look at your soul wounding, so you can finally come to the light!"

Sarah took corn meal into her hands, brought her hands close to her mouth and spoke Light Language into the offering, *"Magodahea paradoda ejahema ehajema, ejahema!"*

Next, Sarah threw the cornmeal into the fire and the flames sprinkled out little fire explosions everywhere. This was a sign for Sarah. Her prayer had been heard. She thanked Fire Spirit and added the wish that all would be done with ease and grace, and Ezrael would receive whatever message he needed.

Master Merlin and Novix were back together and sitting around a fire as well. Both were in deep silence as they felt the energies of light and dark intensifying.

Novix said to Master Merlin, "Today is the day of the days! I feel it in the air!"

A breeze came up as Novix said this.

Master Merlin, very serious today, looked at Novix and replied, "Yes, today is one of the most pivotal days in the history of Planet Earth."

Merlin paused for a while and said, "The Guardian meeting took me by surprise and I am starting to understand why. I might have underestimated how much the dark forces were working against the light without my awareness. In any case, my purpose is to hold the light; the sacred light of Mankind. I know that the humans are ready for the next big step. Mother Gaia is working very hard to stabilize the shifting poles. I can feel it. She is doing an incredible job of aligning constantly to adjust all the energies.

Merlin suggested, "Novix, let us put some offerings into the fire for Mother Gaia, to help and thank her. Everything is truly perfect the way it is. I feel our friend, Ezrael, might need some support from us as well, at this moment."

Merlin with his magic wand in his hand, started to speak, *"Amanaheta Goschtadeha Forasa."*

Next, Master Merlin took magic powder out of his cloak pocket, raised his arms into the air, and shouted, *"Bonawishta Egaheda Maradoschta!"*

Suddenly the wind became stronger. He threw the magic powder into the fire and a huge explosion of light energy burst out of the fire and traveled all around the Earth and the Cosmos.

Ledurah, the Malbecian defense system expert, was meticulously running the final checks on her machines. She and her team were very excited to be working with Occuna on the Solar Eclipse mission. They were thrilled to finally see their prized defense system back up and running, she and her team had worked so hard on.

Soon it would be the time to activate the system with Occuna's code: 5 4, 5, 4, 5, 9, 9. Ledura was proud of serving the Emperor of Darkness and felt like she was finally recognized for her talents and hard work.

Imero and Ammagant were in Imero's study and looked at the black box, which Occuna gave Imero. Ammagant said, "Soon, it will be over and the dark forces will be back in power. I cannot wait and I am really looking forward to us gaining all of our strength back."

Imero looked at Ammagant and replied, "Yes, Ammagant, you speak my mind. I know I can get this done and send out the transmission at the perfect time."

After a short pause, Ammagant said, "Imero, I need to ask you a question."

Imero was curious and replied, "Go ahead, Ammagant."

In the next moment, Ammagant drew a magic bubble around both of them, which he had not done for quite some time. This bubble, Ammagant's own creation, was an energy bubble which allowed them to speak without detection. Even the Emperor of Darkness would not be able to hear them.

Imero was quite surprised about the bubble and knew that whatever Ammagant had to share was crucial and important. Imero was impatiently waiting for Ammagant to speak, and said, "Ammagant speak! Do not keep me waiting!"

Ammagant looked into Imero's eyes with a seriousness Imero had never seen before, and said, "Imero, I do not want to raise any questions and concerns, but I have some repeated thoughts in my mind. I need to share them with you, as I can usually trust what I am getting."

Imero, now really impatient, yelled, "What is it, Ammagant! Tell me NOW!!!!"

Ammagant shared, "What if we cannot trust Occuna? What if Occuna's plan is actually not meant to save Earth? What if his intent is to blow up Earth? As you know, Imero, this would not be the first time he did such a thing. Occuna would get the most power out of an explosion instead of activating a defense system and sending another dark power transmission to Earth."

Imero looked at him and said, "Ammagant, this has crossed my mind as well. What I came to understand is that Earth is of too much value to the whole Cosmos. I do believe that the Guardians would step in, if that was detected by them. As you know, so far, they have always detected everything. We need to follow Occuna's instructions and go full steam ahead. Without the counteract, we will be defeated, and if Earth blows up, we will be defeated as well. So, let us try our best and hope for the best. Right at this moment, we do not have any other choice."

Ammagant had to agree. He was glad he could share his thoughts with Imero. Yes, they were in the same boat, and had no choice other than to fulfill their task ahead.

Most of the Galaxies were not aware that the energies of both dark and light were intensifying and bubbling up. Most humans on Earth, seemed to experience some instability, which was still seen as normal at this point.

However, the Guardians were aware of it all. They were now back in their pure consciousness energy form.

Everything in the Omniverse existed in a pair of two to maintain equilibrium. There was an unseen Divine Intelligent Force, which always worked to achieve balance and harmony. As much dark as there was in the Galaxies, there was also as much light.

Occuna as well, had an equal counterpart of the light. There was someone who existed in the Cosmos, who had not been seen for quite some time. Her name was Serenata and she was the Empress of Light of the Galaxies. For most of her existence, she stayed in her magical tower on the planet of Emuras, far, far away from Earth. Her main work was to send unconditional love and compassion out to the Cosmos. Like Occuna, she existed in pure consciousness form most of the time, and only materialized into physical form when it was needed.

When the Empress of Light, Serenata, was in a physical form, she appeared as a tall, lean woman, with wavy, long, white hair. She always wore a long, white, flowing dress and a crystal on her third eye. Serenata had just received a message from the Guardians and was prepared for action.

Kai, Nina, Olivia and Todd met in town to be part of their town's Solar Eclipse festivities for a little while, before heading to the ceremony at Sarah and Ezrael's house.

Valerie had a busy morning and afternoon helping her parents prepare for a Solar Eclipse party and was hoping she could leave soon.

Ronja needed some alone time and went to the waterfall for meditation and offerings. To her surprise, as she started to meditate, the Sirian Light Beings surrounded her, as they did once before.

Fiandra stepped forward and said, "SumuRa, it is time to claim your power. We are here to help you integrate more of your Lemurian energies."

Ronja was excited and willing. She received the vision of herself in a pyramid. There was an altar right in front of her and on it was an ankh and a crystal pad with numbers on it. The numbers were 66633.

The Sirian, now with her in the vision, instructed her, "Take the crystal pad and repeat the code three times."

Ronja imagined picking up the crystal pad, which was a memory storage unit, and she repeated the code out loud three times, "66633, 66633, 66633."

At the same time, Ezrael, back in his bedroom, meditated to the song. At first, he had a hard time settling down. His mind was racing like a machine, and he did not know how to stop it. Suddenly, he heard a familiar voice saying, "Surrender! Surrender! Surrender! Hodahea aka! Hodahea aka! Hodahea aka!"

In the next moment, he envisioned the energy of the sky flowing through the top of his head and into his heart. While at the same time, all the energies from the Earth were flowing up through his lower chakras into his heart. As these two streams of energies merged in his heart, he finally started to relax and could focus on deep breathing.

Ezrael expected to receive visions of his gifts and powers and was surprised to receive a vision of himself kneeling on the floor in a dark room. He had the heavy feeling of being lost. He was shown many lifetimes where he knew that he was helping others to find the light, while he stayed in total darkness and confusion. Ezrael was overwhelmed by this feeling state and felt his heart was frozen. He experienced a recognition of how he had been sacrificing himself for the sake of others. He was serving the light as a way to find relief from his own soul's suffering. He had to endure many lives in separation and isolation. Reliving these feelings of his own suffering became unbearable for Ezrael. He opened his eyes and threw his cell phone into the corner out of anger and despair.

Ezrael paced around the room, feeling restless and anxious about all the visions he had just received. He decided to walk into the woods to have some alone time. He always felt better connecting to nature and he hoped it would help him feel better today, because he could not bear the feelings he was experiencing.

As soon as he ran into the woods, a wind appeared out of nowhere.

Sarah witnessed Ezrael leaving the house. She continued to sit at the fire and held space for her son. She prayed to the Universe, that through facing his soul's wounding once and for all, he would find his Divinity; the love and light within.

Ronja, still in mediation, felt the wind come up as well. Birds started to sing all around her and she felt energy coming into her body, stronger than she had ever experienced before. As she started breathing deeply, the wind became stronger and stronger. Ronja again saw herself in the pyramid. By surprise, both of her parents appeared to her. Although they looked different, she knew that it was them. Ronja started to cry out of joy to see and feel them again.

In her vision, her father drew a circle in the sand, looked at Ronja and said, "Remember the Cosmic Circle. Remember the Cosmic Circle."

Next, he drew five spokes into the circle and Ronja saw the wheel starting to turn. Suddenly, it created a beam of light energy which flowed into Ronja. Her body started swaying and her vision in the pyramid ended and she was again aware of the Sirian Light Beings surrounding her.

Fiandra spoke again, "The download has been completed. It will take some time to integrate these energies. You will know when the time is right to use the code. We honor you and your willingness. Thank you."

As fast as the Sirian Light Beings appeared, they disappeared. The wind ceased and there was a sacred silence as Ronja opened her eyes.

To Ronja's surprise, she could see a beautiful energy grid. The grid lines were going in vertical and horizontal directions. It was white and silver in color. It was everywhere she could see between the earth and the sky. It appeared to be connecting and flowing through all existence. She reached out to touch it, but her hand went through the grid lines. Ronja was in awe about this magical sight and wondered to herself, "Was this the Crystalline Grid of the Earth?"

Ronja enjoyed her view of this grid all around her for quite a while before it disappeared. Ronja gave thanks for all she had received, gave an offering of tobacco and corn meal to Mother Gaia. Now she knew it was time to go to Sarah's house.

Ezrael arrived at his favorite tree in the woods and kneeled down on the grass underneath it. He could not hold back any longer and cried bitterly. All the feelings of the self-sacrifice and self-sabotage were unbearable. He could not understand how he could feel this way when he only showed kindness and compassion for others. Ezrael had just one thought playing over and over in his mind, "I surrender! I surrender! I surrender! I am willing to feel it all now. I want to release it and finally be free!" Ezrael continued to cry, bent forward, so his forehead could touch the grass.

The wind seemed to blow stronger and he heard animals all around him; sounds he had not heard before. Ezrael just breathed into all the feelings and was willing to intensify them without fear. He asked for help from Spirit and said, "Please help me benevolent Spirits, please help me. I am finally asking for help from you!"

Merlin continued to speak in the Language of Light and added offerings into the fire for Ezrael.

Sarah continued to speak in the Language of Light and added offerings into the fire for Ezrael.

Suddenly, Ezrael felt intense high, benevolent energies coming in, which he had never experienced before and he saw Master Merlin and Novix standing right in front of him.

Master Merlin looked at Ezrael and said in a gentle voice, "Dear Ezrael, thank you for inviting us in. We are always here to support you when you ask us for help. Thank you for surrendering and releasing. We can help you now. What you are not aware of, Ezrael, is that you have always served the light. All souls are beautiful, as is yours. Never forget that. The separation from your Divine Source causes you to suffer, but at the same time, it is this unbearable pain which makes you search for the Divinity within yourself. This is the grand plan. Now, we want to give you the gift of experiencing the full capacity of love, which your soul carries within you. Do you want to receive this gift?"

Ezrael agreed and in the next moment, Merlin pointed his magic wand towards Ezrael and continuously drew a circle in the air, directing it towards Ezrael. This spiraling created an energy vortex, which pulled all the dark energies out of Ezrael. Suddenly, he felt the protective shell around his heart dissolve. He knew he had created this barrier around his heart to avoid deep feelings and getting hurt again.

In this moment, Ezrael felt the feeling of Grace; a feeling of being whole/holy and complete for the first time. He felt the abundance of divine unconditional love and compassion within himself. Ezrael cried, this time out of bliss, and knew that he was part of the Universe and that he was Divine.

In a split second, Merlin and Novix disappeared, and he realized that he felt so much lighter. Ezrael screamed out of joy into the world, "I AM Light! I AM Love! I AM Whole! I AM Complete! I AM Divine!"

Suddenly, the words came out of him, "I know who I am. I know what I am. I know how I serve!" Surprised by his own words, he laughed, got up, gave thanks to nature and to his Spirit Guides, and ran home full of joy.

Master Merlin and Novix, still sitting at the fire, looked at each other and laughed out loud. After a while Novix said, "You are a trickster, sometimes, Merlin."

Merlin grinned and said, "Well, Novix, there are different ways to get humans to see the light, and sometimes we need to surprise them with their healing work, otherwise they would avoid it."

After a pause he continued, "Ezrael is always willing to do his work and I am very proud of him. His transformation is one of the most magical ones to witness, because Ezrael's soul took on the burdens of so many others to bring in the light. And now he has completed this cycle. It is done once and for all! I am excited to see what will happen next. I love and honor this boy so much. He has done great work for this planet, which he is not fully aware of, yet. Love will show him the way. I do trust that he will not only know, but also really feel soon, that love is all there is!"

Both became silent and stared into the mystical fire. Yes, transformation was in the air.

CHAPTER 21

The Day of the Solar Eclipse

It was almost 3 pm in the afternoon, and all except Valerie had already arrived at Sarah's house for the gathering. The sky was clear of clouds and perfect for viewing the Eclipse. Everyone was excited. Todd, Nina, Kai, Ronja, Olivia, Sarah and Ezrael were gathered outside around the fire. After they shared their experiences from the last two days with each other, they decided not to waste any time and started to meditate around the fire. At 3:33 pm the total Solar Eclipse would be witnessed and total darkness would be present for three minutes.

Valerie had finally finished helping her parents and was only few blocks away from Sarah's house. She texted Ronja that she would be there very soon.

Imero and Ammagant were in Imero's study and waited with some apprehension about starting Occuna's transmission.

Ledura had just finished the final checkup for her devices. All worked properly and she was excited about the task ahead.

Occuna, now safely hidden away in his own dark kingdom, was excited to see the outcome from the blast of his device.

Ammagant and Imero were right, he had other plans in store for Earth and the Galaxies. Occuna had created another device, which he held in his hand. He was waiting for the Solar Eclipse to happen and in the perfect moment of total darkness, he was going to blow up the Earth and receive the ultimate power from this magical planet's destruction. Occuna could already feel the rush of this power and had to laugh out loud.

Kamit, the King and the Queen of the Reptilians, gathered in their royal chambers in Inner Earth. All were excited to witness the defeat of the light forces with Occuna's dark invention during the Solar Eclipse. The Queen, Kafura, was ready to employ her own dark plan, which she had been waiting to do for a long time.

She looked at both and said, "It is time! I shall proceed to support the return of my Kingdom." In the next moment, she sat on her throne, closed her eyes and started to send out her dark energies to the surface of the Earth, which she rarely had to do. The Queen had immense powers. She started to make a sound, which sounded like the buzzing of a bee.

Valerie decided to take a short cut to Sarah's house. Instead of walking on the path, she walked through a beautiful flower meadow. She saw the house in front of her and was glad to be arriving in time.

Suddenly, she heard an unusually loud buzzing sound and wondered where it was coming from. A moment later, she felt a sting on her right leg and looked down and saw that a bee had stung her. "That is weird," she thought. Although she was not usually paranoid, she immediately picked up her phone and called Ronja.

Ronja answered the phone and Valerie told her about the bee sting and that she was in the meadow, right in front of Sarah's house. She told Ronja that she was not allergic to bees, however, she had a strong feeling that this could be interference. She asked if Ronja could walk towards her quickly, so she would not be alone, just in case something happened. Ronja agreed right away.

Ronja shared this news with the group and Ezrael immediately volunteered to join her. Sarah got up right away and said, "I have a homeopathic remedy in the house for bee stings and I will give you some ice to take with you." Sarah ran inside, got the items, and handed them to Ronja. She instructed them how to use the remedy, and both went on their way to meet Valerie.

Valerie felt so relieved when she saw Ronja and Ezrael appear at the other side of the meadow. She waved at them and both waved back. In the next moment, Valerie became very weak and was not able to move forward. A sudden, chilling feeling went through her whole body and Valerie collapsed.

Ronja and Ezrael saw Valerie collapsing in the meadow. They were only 40 feet away from her. Ronja started to scream, "Valerie! Valerie! Oh my God! Valerie! Come on Ezrael, we need to run!"

It was only a couple minutes away from the total Solar Eclipse. The energies on Planet Earth had started to shift. The animal kingdom became quiet and silence was felt everywhere. The light on Earth had started to decrease.

Occuna was excited and totally focused on Earth. He knew the power of thought and imagined the beautiful destruction of Earth. Suddenly, he felt the energy of a visitor. An energy he had not felt for a very long time.

His entire kingdom started to shake and Serenata, The Empress of Light, appeared right in front of him.

Novix and Merlin, still sitting around the fire, watched in joy as Light Beings from the forest came towards them from all directions. Elves, Unicorns, Dragons, Fairies, Centaurs, Golden Dolphins, Whales and other nature spirits joined them. They all gathered around the fire in silence.

Merlin and Novix looked at each other and said, "The time has come!"

Imukah, at the Central Sun Transmission station, started to send down the high, benevolent frequencies to Earth, as planned.

It was getting darker and darker as the total eclipse was only minutes away. Sarah had started the ceremony with her usual opening. They all held hands and knew what to do. Sarah held space for Valerie, Ezrael and Ronja. She knew that they had to start the ceremony without them and that Ezrael and Ronja were meant to help Valerie during this time.

A few seconds after Valerie collapsed to the ground, she lost consciousness. Her Spirit traveled to Inner Earth and she found herself standing in front of the Queen Kafura, who was sitting on her throne.

The Queen came down from her thrown and said to Valerie (Maheta), "Maheta, my Dear! Welcome to my Kingdom! I have waited to meet you for quite some time and now it is the time. I am glad you answered the calling of my invite."

The Queen Kafura felt so good about herself and had to laugh about her grandiose plan.

Maheta looked at the Queen and said in a stern voice, "No more bad behavior! You have done your damage on Earth and now it is time for you to leave. You are done here!"

The Queen replied with laughter, "Oh, my dear Maheta, you are speaking the words out of my mind, which I am here to tell YOU!"

She walked towards Maheta and started to look sternly into her eyes and said, "Dear sister of ours, don't you remember you were one of us? I will help you remember. Kafura looked even more fiercely into Valerie's eyes and Valerie felt frozen as she received a transmission from the Queen.

Valerie saw herself ruling the kingdom of the Reptilians and remembered all the power she had during that time.

Serenata, the Empress of Light, appeared in front of Occuna.

With disgust he spit on the floor and said, "What a marvelously disgusting visitor I am receiving!"

He felt her powerful light energy, which made him even more irritated.

Serenata walked towards Occuna, looked straight into his eyes and said with compassion, "Dear friend, I am here to ask you to stop your plan of destroying the Earth. You know this cannot be allowed, Occuna. It is time for you to merge with me and surrender to love and light; the secret desire you have had throughout your existence. As you know, we are extremely powerful opposites and together we can become an even more powerful Union. Together we can create magical Galaxies."

Occuna looked at her with so much hatred. He could not stand the intense light energies of Serenata. He was aware that he looked at his opposite, the one of equal powers of the other side. He was intrigued by the idea of increasing his energy capacities, yet, he would never be willing to share his ruling power. He truly hated every moment of standing beside her.

Ronja and Ezrael finally reached Valerie. She was lying on the ground and was unresponsive. Ronja, who thankfully had attended many First Aid classes, knew what to do. She checked for a pulse and made sure she was still breathing. Thankfully, Valerie was breathing and had a pulse. She asked Ezrael to call 911, which he did. Ronja followed the guidelines she learned and put Valerie on her side. She found the swollen bee sting site on her right leg and put ice on it. Next, she put the homeopathic pellets for bee sting into Valerie's mouth, as Sarah had instructed.

The fully dark time of the Solar Eclipse had started on Earth.

Ledura put in the code, which Occuna gave her, and suddenly the machines started to become loud and her office started to shake a little. The transmission had started and the dark force's defense system was up and running successfully.

Imero looked at Ammagant with a smile and said, "It is time!" He pressed the button, and everything in Imero's study started to shake.

The Queen Kafura was continuing to stare into Maheta's eyes. She was working on shifting Valerie's DNA to 100% Reptilian. Maheta had 30% Reptilian DNA to begin with, as it was her mission in this life to heal and transmute this to 0%. Through only a few minutes of the powerful energy transmission from the Queen, Valerie's reptilian DNA had already increased to 70%.

The Queen said to Maheta, "You will be a wonderful disciple of mine. With all your powers, you will help me bring my kingdom back." The Queen of the Reptilians started to laugh hysterically, not taking her eyes off Valerie.

Sarah and the Star Team, still holding the field of the ceremony, felt all the dark energies being bombarded into their field. They continued toning and speaking Light Language. They all knew that they had full support of all benevolent Light Beings to help transmute the dark energies. In that moment, the Star Team received an important insight, "Ask, and you shall receive." This was the secret of free will on the planet. The pure intent was all which was needed to activate the support of all dimensional, benevolent beings.

Sarah asked all of them to speak the Cosmic Language of Light at the same time. The energies increased, and all of a sudden, they all felt a beautiful shift of energy and the Star Team knew, that they had accomplished their task.

Suddenly, Sarah said, "Ceremony is over. Let's go!"

They all felt the same way and started running towards the meadow with flashlights, so they would be able to see in the dark.

Merlin, Novix and all the Light Beings, who still were gathered around the fire, started to tone together. Their sounds created the most beautiful angelic symphony that had ever been heard in the history of the Omniverse.

Ezrael and Ronja, who kneeled on either side of Valerie, waited impatiently for the EMT to arrive. Ezrael turned on his flashlight so Ronja could continue to monitor Valerie's vital signs. They were relieved when Valerie started to moan and move a little bit. Ronja gave Valerie another dose of the homeopathic remedy.

Ronja and Ezrael felt intense energies coming in as the darkness of the full Solar Eclipse was upon them. To Ezrael's surprise, his newly acquired gift of sight had stopped and he could no longer see the energy fields.

He said to Ronja, "My sight is gone. I do not see anymore."

Ronja, in her mind's eye, saw all the Light Beings appear, forming a circle around them. She said to Ezrael, "Trust, Ezrael! All our Guides are here. I can see them around us now."

Ezrael felt intense energies coming in and started to breathe deeply. Suddenly he started to have visions again in his inner mind.

As Ronja put her hands on Valerie to give her some energy, her parents appeared in front of her. Although she was so excited to see them, she started to feel all the grief again, which she thought she had healed already. She started to cry bitterly and Ezrael, who was in his own intense process, just knew that he had to hold her hands. Even though, he was unable to speak, he knew he needed to comfort her in this way. So he put his hands on top of Ronja's hands.

Ronja's Mom said, "It is time that you open your heart again, Ronja. You have expanded so much out into the spirit world. Protecting your heart and not being fully in your body will hinder your evolution, Ronja. Come back into your body and open your heart. All the gifts you have acquired from Spirit, will be with you always."

In the next moment, Ronja felt intense energies in her heart. She was suddenly so aware of how she had escaped out into the spirit world, because it gave her so much bliss and peace. She was not really in her physical body due to the pain which was held there. She realized how much she did not accept her physical form. She did not feel that she was beautiful and she realized how much she self-sabotaged by judging herself as not being good enough.

Her father stepped forward and said, "Integrate everything in your body now. You are meant to be on Earth, not only in the other worlds. Your power comes from the compassionate heart and being open to all there is in the 3D world. Vulnerability is one of the keys for Ascension. It is necessary to be open to experience the raw feelings of emotions and then deal with them in a compassionate way. This creates authenticity. When you love, like you have never been hurt before, you shall receive the magic of the Cosmic Heart."

Her father continued, "We have never left you. This is an illusion. We are in your DNA and part of your soul. We all are ONE in truth and only LOVE is real. When you understand this law of the Cosmic Circle of the Stars, Ronja, you will feel your divine wholeness and connection with all there is. You will no longer feel abandoned or hurt, nor fear death."

Suddenly, emerald green energies were flowing from all the Light Beings into Ronja, Valerie and Ezrael. Ronja saw a spinning circle of energy appear.

Ezrael felt intense energies coming in and started to breathe deeply. He started to have visions in his mind's eye. He received flashes from many lifetimes, almost simultaneously. He remembered how he was killed in so many lifetimes because he was serving the light. Ezrael felt overwhelmed and started to cry. He re-lived the emotions of being alone, being defeated, being lied to, being betrayed by others who were pretending to love him, when they just wanted to steal his gifts. By surprise, at the same time, Ezrael felt his light, his power, forgiveness and compassion in his heart.

Ronja, now feeling the grief and pain of coming back into her body, suddenly started to get visions of her many traumatic past lives as well. She flashed through the many times she was killed, outlawed, abandoned and deceived for carrying the light. The emotions she felt became too much for her to handle, and Ronja said, "Dear parents and Light Beings, please help me! I surrender!"

Suddenly, Ronja saw herself becoming a beam of light, and started feeling aligned to all her multidimensional soul aspects. Finally, she could see her soul's beauty, and how she had impacted the lives of so many others with her compassionate heart and light.

Ronja, feeling better for now, became aware of her surroundings again, and saw Ezrael starting to shake a little bit, and she knew he was struggling.

With an overwhelming feeling of compassion in her heart now, she said to Ezrael, "Look into my left eye, Ezrael! Look into my eye!"

Despite feeling the fear of intimacy and being vulnerable, she knew that she had to step out of the box now. That this was the opportunity.

Ezrael listened to Ronja and looked into her left eye. When their eyes connected, instantly both felt their hearts blast open and beautiful, golden and emerald energies were creating infinity symbols around and within their hearts.

Suddenly, Ezrael saw himself back in the pyramid again, with the woman, who was now showing him the dragons on her palms again. In a flash of a second, he saw himself and Ronja flying through the Cosmos. He was riding on a red dragon and Ronja on a green dragon.

He said to Ronja, "Oh my God, it is you! You are the one I am supposed to remember! It is you!" Ezrael felt very excited, and his heart opened up even more.

All the dark energies continued to flow into Earth and could be felt everywhere. Occuna's transmission was working.

Ronja did not know what to do with the shyness starting to come up, and she diverted her attention back to Valerie, realizing it was time to check her vital signs. Valerie seemed to be stable, although she was still not awake. She was groaning and mumbling, now and then. Ronja gave her undivided attention to Valerie.

Ezrael sat at the other side of Valerie, put his hands on top of Ronja's hands, in hope of getting the connection back with Ronja.

Ronja, feeling shy and vulnerable, said in a defensive tone, "I told you that I was supposed to find you in this life and I did. Who cares about the connection we had. It all does not matter. Just because we have a past life connection it does not mean anything. We have connections with many people."

Ezrael suddenly got flashes of a life they had together back in Lemuria. He remembered how they had hundreds of years together, and at the same time, he saw flashes of their lifetimes as Mayans in Mexico, holding many ceremonies and working together in service for the people as well.

Ezrael said to Ronja, "We had to meet for a reason. You know we agreed to come back to Earth together to help each other. You found me and I am thankful for it. We all have been hurt. We all have endured pain. Now, I am starting to understand that if we truly find the divine within ourselves, we feel whole and no longer need anything outside of us to make us happy. When feeling this connection, we release all fears and can be present in every moment with confidence. Somehow, you are also helping me to remember myself. I am kind. I am generous and always willing to be of service, like you, Ronja."

As Ronja listened to Ezrael, something shifted. She felt the love energy of the cosmic circle in her heart. She started to remember the sacred teachings of the Cosmic Circle, that was a gift from the Stars, to help humans to evolve in consciousness, and to find God within. She remembered the feeling of Divine love, compassion and Oneness.

As she surrendered to these beautiful energies coming in, Ronja felt her heart soften and she could finally relax. She said to Ezrael, "I think what I am feeling at the moment, Ezrael, is what every soul has deep inside. When we find our own light within, we can see it in others. I wish that every human could have the chance to experience this sacredness."

This time, Ronja put her hands on top of Ezrael's, which were on Valerie, and said, "Thank you, friend. You do not know how much you just helped me."

Ezrael had a little grin on his face, looked into Ronja's eyes, and said, "You are welcome. I am so glad I could be of service too."

Suddenly, Ezrael's sight came back and for a moment he was confused by what he was seeing. All three of them were in the Lemurian pyramid. He knew that this was not a vision. It seemed so real that he was wondering if they suddenly were teletransported into a different timeline.

Ezrael said to Ronja, "Oh my God. We are in Lemuria as we speak. I do not understand what is going on. All I can say is that we ARE in the Lemurian pyramid. This IS the pyramid, I had many visions about earlier. You were in those visions as well."

Ronja (Yaheema), who experienced the same, looked at Ezrael (Yahee) with a smile and spoke in a soft voice, *"Godnoahadeha aka. Manobahedo Odagostahada Enaaheja aka!"*

She started to laugh and continued with joy, *"Manaheta Godo Ehagodonaheda aka. Heyja Doda Manahesto Ogaheda Nodamaka!"*

Maheta, (Valerie), still staring into the Queen of the Reptilian's eyes, was holding her own against the Queen, and the frozen feeling in her body was starting to diminish. Suddenly, the Queen was distracted by a beam of light that came in and surrounded Maheta. The Queen felt a weakening of her power, as these beautiful light energies flowed to her from Maheta. Kamit and the King recognized the danger and moved closer to support the Queen energetically. They had no doubt that the powerful Queen would overcome this little obstacle.

Suddenly, Maheta bilocated into a parallel timeline, in which she was in a pure light consciousness form. All the Divine energies of love and compassion flowed from this pure consciousness timeline into her being in the Inner Earth timeline, where Maheta was engaging with the Queen. The only thoughts Maheta had repeating over and over in her mind were, "I know who I Am! I know what I Am! I know how I Serve! I know who We Are! I know what We Are! I know how We Serve!"

Ronja, who was still speaking in the Language of Light, suddenly heard Valerie mumbling words out loud, "YES! I know who I Am! I know what I Am! I know how I Serve! I know who We Are! I know what We Are! I know how We Serve!"

Ezrael, hearing Valerie's words, saw a beam of light appear from above. The portal of light surrounded Valerie, Ronja, himself and all the Cosmic Light Beings.

All of a sudden, Ronja heard her father saying, "She is the Guardian! She is the Guardian! She is the Guardian!"

Ronja did not understand the meaning of this message, as she had never heard of "the Guardian" before.

Imero and Ammagant felt their powers coming back and enjoyed the energies. In addition, to assure maximum impact, Ammagant and Imero were guided to send their dark energies to Earth as well.

The Star Team saw Ezrael's flashlight in the meadow and that the ambulance was just arriving to the edge of the meadow behind them. The closer the Star Team got to Valerie, Ezrael and Ronja, the harder it was for them to move forward. They were almost there. They were almost there.

Serenate looked at Occuna with compassion and said, "I love you! I am so sorry! Please forgive me!

Thank you! We are ONE! *Ehadaheeeee! Deda aheeee! Hodonada aheeee! Edidoda Ahee!"*

Serenata radiated out the pure white light of love as she spoke.

Occuna flinched in hatred at every word she said. He was not willing to give in to the merge and be defeated by this disgusting energy, called "Divine Love". He knew how to withstand love and light, as he had done so, since the beginning of his existence.

Occuna's entire kingdom started to shake, due to the immensely powerful energies, created by Serenata. Despite his resistance, Occuna started to weaken and fell on the ground. His destruction device fell out of Occuna's hands and onto the floor, just out of his reach.

Serenata continued to blast out the love energy while repeating the words, "I love you! I am so sorry! Please forgive me! Thank you! *Ehadaheeeee! Deda aheeee! Hodonada aheeee! Edidoda ahee!"*

Occuna started to shake and felt frozen for a second.

Ledura was quite excited as the new defense system had neutralized the Rainbow Bridge and was now connected to Occuna's transmission. Everything was running beautifully, as Occuna had promised.

Merlin, Novix and all the Light Beings continued and intensified their toning around the fire.

While Imukah's high frequency transmission reached full power, Imukah worked on reversing the neutralization of the Rainbow Bridge.

As Valerie continued to repeat the words, her voice became stronger and louder. Although they were in the portal of light, Ronja and Ezrael felt the dark energies intensify.

Ronja received a flash of knowing, looked at Ezrael, and said with a courageous tone, "Just do it, Ezrael! Just do it! You know what to do, NOW! It is all here! It is all here for you to claim!"

Ezrael said with authority, "Okay, I claim all my powers and gifts, NOW, with Love and Compassion!"

He immediately saw the Divine Crystalline Matrix appear all around them. He felt the connection of being one with the Grid, the Divine Intelligence, where all knowledge, including the remembrance of all his gifts, was stored.

Ezrael opened his arms wide, looked to the sky and started to speak, in a deep powerful voice, *"MAGADAHOOOOODAAAAAA EKTA AHEEEEEDA GODOBISCH!!!! FADARAHEA OKTUNABETA GODOHA! ENAMAMISCHTA HODANAHEDA OGADABAHEDA!"*

Suddenly a storm appeared and heavy winds started to blow.

Ronja gave Valerie a kiss on her cheek and was guided to say to her, "You are the Guardian! You are the Guardian! You are the Guardian! It is time for you to remember how powerful you are! NOW!"

The Star Team finally arrived and kneeled down with Ezrael and Ronja, forming a circle around Valerie. They knew that something extremely important was taking place at this time and held space in silence. They were all thankful to be united again.

Back in Inner Earth, Maheta, hearing Ronja's voice telling her she was the Guardian, said to the Queen, "I love you! We are all ONE! I love you! We are but ONE! You are me and I am you and I have compassion for myself and for you!"

The Queen Kafura, repulsed by Maheta's words, screamed, "You will be MINE! You will be MINE! Forget this light and love! I choose the DARK! I choose the dark side! I AM THE DARK! As I will ALWAYS BE!"

Kafura's ranting had no impact on Maheta. Maheta only felt a deep sense of compassion and love for her dark sided sister. She was aware that the Queen and all the beings of the dark had agreed to play their roles for the highest good of all, in accordance with the Divine's Plan. Every being on the planet was here to remember Divine love.

By choosing compassion and love, Maheta had just received the miracle of transmuting all of her Reptilian's DNA. She initiated the quantum potential, starting the irreversible domino effect for all the Reptilian DNA to be transmuted as well. The mission, which she had come to fulfill in this lifetime, was complete.

Occuna, using his own dark energies to support himself, unfroze quickly and could move a little again. The Emperor of Darkness had just enough energy to move within reach of the device and brought the Earth destruction device back into his hands.

Occuna looked at Serenata, started to laugh hysterically and screamed, "I AM THE EMPEROR OF THE GALAXIES! I AM THE EMPEROR OF DARKNESS! MY WISH IS MY COMMAND!"

Serenata, smiling calmly, was filled with compassion for her dark counterpart, continued to beam light and love from her heart towards him.

Occuna, even more irritated by her response, continued, "I am here to gain power and make you all feel small and insignificant! God has created me for a reason, and I am here on my own mission, to serve ME!"

Valerie, suddenly regained consciousness and opened her eyes to see all of her new-found friends around her. She had an "Inner Knowing" that something needed to be done immediately.

In the next moment, she felt a bolt of energy flowing through her, raised her hand to the sky and started to speak in the Language of Light for the first time, *"Vodaheda Mangoka Venahischna Kopura!"*

The wind intensified and created a tornado right above them. A white light shot from Valerie's hand up into the sky.

Occuna, suddenly became surprisingly calm and said, "I am now becoming God! I am God and I will rule for the rest of time! There is nothing you can do! I have created the Quantum Field! I know how to create! I am the Master and EARTH IS DONE! Yes, Earth is done for all!!! He looked at Serenata, started to laugh out loud and pressed the button...

....to be continued.

CPSIA information can be obtained
at www.ICGtesting.com
Printed in the USA
BVHW06s1118230518
517123BV00010B/132/P

9 781948 817509